THE EXCHANGE RATE SYSTEM

THE EXCHANGE RATE SYSTEM

John Williamson

INSTITUTE FOR INTERNATIONAL ECONOMICS
WASHINGTON, DC
SEPTEMBER 1983. Revised JUNE 1985

Dr. John Williamson is a Senior Fellow at the Institute for International Economics. He was formerly economics professor at Pontifícia Universidade Católica do Rio de Janeiro, University of Warwick, Massachusetts Institute of Technology, University of York, and Princeton University; Advisor to the International Monetary Fund; and Economic Consultant to Her Majesty's Treasury. Dr. Williamson has published numerous studies on international monetary issues, including *IMF Conditionality, Exchange Rate Rules,* and *The Failure of World Monetary Reform, 1971–74.*

The author wishes to acknowledge the many helpful comments on earlier drafts that he has received from members of the Board of Directors and Advisory Committee of the Institute for International Economics, as well as from colleagues. J. W.

INSTITUTE FOR INTERNATIONAL ECONOMICS
C. Fred Bergsten, *Director*
Kathleen A. Lynch, *Director of Publications*

Published September 1983. Second edition June 1985.

The Institute for International Economics was created, and is principally funded, by The German Marshall Fund of the United States.

The views expressed in this publication are those of the author. The publication is part of the overall program of the Institute, as endorsed by its Board of Directors, but does not necessarily reflect the views of individual members of the Board or the Advisory Committee.

Library of Congress Cataloging in Publications Data

Williamson, John, 1937–
    The exchange rate system.

    (Policy analyses in international economics; 5)
    "September 1983."
    Bibliography: p. 92
    1. Foreign exchange problem. I. Institute for
International Economics (U.S.) II. Title. III. Series.
HG3851.W534 1985   332.4'5   85–11975
ISBN 0–88132–034–X

Contents

TEXT TABLES

TEXT FIGURE

Preface

The Institute first released this important study of the exchange rate system in September 1983. The study had three major purposes: to demonstrate the feasibility of calculating "fundamental equilibrium exchange rates" for the major currencies, to apply those techniques to show the extent of contemporary misalignment in the exchange markets, and to elaborate on a "target zone" system that might help prevent such misalignments in the future. The study, and others on the same themes, generated considerable discussion including an "official" response from the United States Treasury Department.

This new edition updates the analysis in two ways. First, John Williamson recalculates the "fundamental equilibrium exchange rates" as of late 1984 (rather than early 1983, as in the original) and compares his results with those of several other observers of the same phenomena—all of whom conclude that the misalignments have become considerably greater than in the previous calculations. Second, the author responds to several comments on his original presentation, particularly covering the feasibility of designing and implementing a "target zone" system of exchange rate management.

The Institute for International Economics is a private nonprofit research institution for the study and discussion of international economic policy. Its purpose is to analyze important issues in that area and to develop and communicate practical new approaches for dealing with them.

The Institute was created in November 1981 through a generous commitment of funds from the German Marshall Fund of the United States. Support is being received from other private foundations and corporations, and the Institute is now broadening and diversifying its financial base.

The Board of Directors bears overall responsibility for the Institute and gives general guidance and approval to its research program—including identification of topics that are likely to become important to international economic policymakers over the medium run (generally, one to three years) and which thus should be addressed by the Institute. The Director of the Institute, working closely with the staff and outside Advisory Committee, is

7

responsible for the development of particular projects and makes the final decision to publish an individual study. The Institute is completely nonpartisan.

The Institute hopes that its studies and other activities will contribute to building a stronger foundation for international economic policy around the world. Comments as to how it can best do so are invited from readers of these publications.

C. FRED BERGSTEN
Director
June 1985

8

1 Introduction

Exchange rates among the world's principal currencies have now floated for over a decade. That is sufficient time to have established beyond doubt that floating rates display a great deal of variability and that the adoption of floating does not resolve all balance of payments problems. Whether it would be possible to do better than the present system of "unstructured floating," neither free nor managed according to systematic principles, is the key question addressed in this study.

The move to floating rates in 1973 was welcomed, with varying degrees of enthusiasm, by most economists. Many had been arguing the desirability of greater flexibility for years, and even those who would have preferred limited flexibility—a combination of a wide band and a crawling peg— breathed a sigh of relief when the attempt to prop up the adjustable peg[1] was abandoned. The dire predictions of the consequences of floating that were voiced by defenders of the *status quo ante* before the event, regarding a prospective seize-up of the foreign exchange markets and major disruptions to trade, failed to materialize.

But the demonstration that floating is *viable* has not been matched by a consensus that it is *desirable*. Instead, more and more observers have been alarmed by the violent swings in exchange rates among the floating currencies—swings dramatically bigger than anything experienced by the Canadian dollar in the 1950s, which provided the experiment with floating that nurtured support in the 1960s.

In assessing the implications of the observed variability in floating exchange rates, it is important to distinguish between short-term *volatility* and persistent *misalignments*. By volatility is meant the amount of short-run variability in

---

1. The "adjustable peg" is the most apt term for the Bretton Woods exchange rate system, under which exchange rates were normally maintained within a narrow band around a fixed par value—but that par value or "peg" might occasionally be discretely adjusted, in a devaluation or revaluation.

the exchange rate from hour to hour, day to day, week to week, or month to month. By misalignment is meant a persistent departure of the exchange rate from its long-run equilibrium level. These two dimensions of variability are distinct, for rates can be volatile around an equilibrium level of competitiveness or stable over long periods while misaligned. The first part of this study seeks to provide measures of both these dimensions of variability. Measuring misalignments is difficult and the measures are inherently imprecise, since they require estimation of what is termed the "fundamental equilibrium exchange rate" (abbreviated, with apologies, to FEER). Estimates are presented for recent misalignments of the five major currencies that compose the SDR.

The next section presents the case for a degree of management of the exchange rate designed to limit misalignments. It discusses the costs of both volatility and misalignments and argues that the past failure of economists to make this distinction has led to the major costs—those of misalignments—being overlooked. An attempt is also made to identify what is sacrificed by attempting to manage rates, as opposed to either fixing them or allowing them to float freely, and argues that those sacrifices are likely to be much less than the benefits of limiting misalignments provided that two conditions are satisfied. The first is that it proves possible to recognize misalignments, at least when they are large. The second is that the country has a convincing alternative anchor to control inflation, such as a determination to orient general macroeconomic policy to that end.

The fourth section considers alternative possible arrangements for systematically managing exchange rates with a view to limiting misalignments. It is argued that this would require an attempt to determine fundamental equilibrium exchange rates and a commitment to orient monetary policy at least in part toward discouraging excessive deviations from those "target" rates. The range within which deviations are not judged to be excessive is called a "target zone," although the term is used with some hesitation because it seems to be associated by some with a considerably more rigid system than that advocated in this study.

The final section discusses the role of surveillance by the International Monetary Fund (IMF) in negotiating and subsequently adjusting a set of agreed target zones among the major currencies, and supervising the consistency of countries' monetary-fiscal policies with their target zones.

2   Measures of Exchange Rate Variability

As argued above, it is important to distinguish the two dimensions of variability, which are now often referred to as volatility and misalignments.

Volatility

One can conceive of two alternative approaches to measuring volatility. The first would be to seek the typical change in the rate from one period (hour, day, week, or month) to the next. This approach has traditionally been employed by the IMF. Summarizing recent findings, the Fund states (IMF, 1983, p. 9n):

The increased flexibility of members' exchange arrangements in the 1970s as compared with the Bretton Woods system is evident from a comparison of the average magnitudes of exchange rate changes in the period January 1948–August 1971, and in the subsequent period through the end of 1981. For the Fund membership as a whole, the average monthly change (without regard to sign) rose fourfold, from 0.3 percent in the former period to 1.4 percent in the latter. . . . The increase in flexibility was more marked for the group of industrial countries, for which average monthly changes increased almost tenfold, from 0.2 percent to 1.9 percent.

The other approach is to seek the typical deviation of the rate from its short-run moving average. The natural measure of volatility under this approach is the coefficient of variation (standard deviation divided by mean) of exchange rates quoted at frequent intervals around a moving average. Rates quoted at frequent intervals cannot meaningfully be corrected for inflation, since price indices are published relatively infrequently, so the calculation is done in terms of *nominal* exchange rates. Similarly, what matter in the short-run decisions on which volatility impinges are *bilateral* rates against a particular currency, and especially against the major vehicle currency, the US dollar, rather than average—i.e., *effective*—exchange rates. Table 1 therefore compares the coefficient of variation of the other major currencies around a six-month moving average in the final years of the

TABLE 1   **Exchange rate volatility under pegged and floating exchange rates**

	1968	1969	1975	1982
Deutschemark	0.3	1.2[a]	1.7	1.6
French franc	0.1	2.3[a]	1.6	2.2
Japanese yen	n.a.	n.a.	0.7	2.5
Pound sterling	0.7[a]	0.2	1.0	1.1

n.a. Not available.
Note: Coefficient of variation of daily nominal exchange rate against dollar around six-month moving average, expressed as percentage.
Source: IMF *International Financial Statistics.*
a. Figure was influenced by a par value change.

Bretton Woods system,[2] in the first year of floating for which data are available, and in 1982.

It can be seen that exchange rate volatility in the Bretton Woods period was very sensitive to par value changes. In 1969 the French franc was devalued and the DM was revalued, and in consequence volatility was substantial. Similarly, the measure of sterling volatility in 1968 reflects the sterling devaluation of late 1967. In years when there was no par value change, volatility was small, an average of 0.2 percent. Under floating, volatility is regularly as large as it used to be in the years of par value changes under the Bretton Woods system, an average of close to 2 percent. Since par value changes were infrequent occurrences, it is clear that volatility on this measure has increased greatly since the advent of floating, by a factor of between 5 and 10, just as on the IMF measure. Moreover, volatility has, if anything, increased since the early years of floating, rather than diminishing as the markets gained experience. The conclusions that the increase in volatility is not sensitive to the particular measures chosen, and that volatility has increased since the mid-1970s, are consistent with the findings of Kenen and Rodrik (1983) and Shafer and Loopesko (1983).

It must be recognized, however, that other things besides the exchange rate regime changed between the late 1960s and the early 1980s. In particular, technological advances in telecommunications led to far closer links between the main markets, which enabled news to have an instantaneous worldwide impact on financial markets. Those advances occurred virtually simultaneously

2. Data were not available for 1970.

with the breakdown of the Bretton Woods system, so there is no easy test of the extent to which technological progress rather than floating may have been responsible for the increase in volatility that is shown by the data. In addition there has been a marked increase in capital mobility, resulting in part from the liberalization of capital controls in the United States in 1974, in Britain in 1979, and in Japan in 1980.

Misalignment

A misalignment was defined above as a "persistent departure of the exchange rate from its long-run equilibrium level." It is necessary to justify this definition and to explain why one may usefully regard a rate as being misaligned even though it may clear the market (i.e., equate demand and supply). The most convenient way of doing that is to distinguish three concepts of equilibrium.[3]

MARKET EQUILIBRIUM   This is simply the exchange rate that balances demand and supply in the absence of official intervention. This concept refers to the nominal rather than the real exchange rate, and tends to change rapidly whenever some relevant "news" changes. It is relatively easy to identify the presence of equilibrium in this sense, since the objective fact of nonintervention[4] implies that the rate is in equilibrium. Conversely, absence of equilibrium is signified by heavy intervention and perhaps reserve borrowing intended to sustain the rate. This concept of equilibrium is sometimes taken to be the only relevant concept by those of a monetarist persuasion.

FUNDAMENTAL EQUILIBRIUM   This term is intended to connote the obverse of "fundamental disequilibrium," the criterion for an exchange rate change under the Bretton Woods system. Although the term was never formally

---

3. The following discussion draws on Bergsten and Williamson (1983). The three-way classification suggested there has subsequently been extended to a five-level classification by Armington and Wolford (1983), who add "current underlying equilibrium" and "underlying equilibrium," but these concepts are not relevant for present purposes.

4. An element of ambiguity does, however, enter through the existence of government transactions. The usual resort is to define nonintervention as a situation where the government does not seek to alter the timing of its transactions with a view to influencing the exchange rate.

defined, the IMF's (1970) report on the exchange rate system implied that fundamental disequilibrium was a situation in which a country could not expect to generate a current account balance to match its underlying capital flow over the cycle as a whole without, on the one hand, depressing its income below "internal balance" or imposing trade controls for payments purposes or, on the other hand, importing inflation. Conversely, therefore, the fundamental equilibrium exchange rate is that which is expected to generate a current account surplus or deficit equal to the underlying capital flow over the cycle,[5] given that the country is pursuing "internal balance" as best it can and not restricting trade for balance of payments reasons. This second concept is what is often meant by "the rate justified by fundamentals." It is also what people usually have in mind when they describe rates as "overvalued" or "undervalued"—and it is used in that sense in this study.

The fact that a rate can become overvalued when a country inflates faster than its partners makes it obvious that this concept of an equilibrium rate relates not to the nominal exchange rate but rather to the *real* rate—i.e., the exchange rate adjusted for inflation at home and in competitor countries. Another term sometimes used to describe the FEER is the "purchasing power parity" or "PPP rate"—an expression that has been resisted here because of its unjustifiable suggestion that relative price levels *alone* are sufficient to pin down the long-run equilibrium level of the exchange rate. *Other things being equal*, however, one expects the nominal exchange rate consistent with long-run or fundamental equilibrium to change in accord with differential inflation, as posited by PPP theory.

The fundamental equilibrium exchange rate may change either because the underlying capital flow changes or because of changes in the pattern of demand for, or conditions of supply of, traded goods. Changes in underlying capital flows can on occasion be important: for example, when a country like Brazil gains access to the international capital market (in the early 1970s) or loses its creditworthiness (in the early 1980s). Whether one should also adjust the FEER to reflect the changes in capital flows that result from such

---

5. Adoption of this definition for the FEER is in no way inconsistent with the fact that the vast bulk (probably over 90 percent) of the value of all exchange market transactions is on capital rather than current account, or with a belief that the *market* rate is determined by the views of wealth owners as postulated in the "asset market approach" to the explanation of exchange rates. (See Williamson, 1983, ch. 10 for an exposition of the asset market approach and references to the literature.)

fiscal developments as the emergence of a structural budget deficit in the United States is a difficult question, discussed later in this section.

Changes in demand and supply which affect long-run real equilibrium exchange rates go on all the time, but those large enough to have a perceptible macroeconomic impact seem to fall into three categories. First, differential productivity growth in different countries means that a fast-growing country like Japan will need some real appreciation over time.[6] Such changes are, however, gradual. Second, exploitation of important new resource discoveries—like North Sea oil—may permit a real appreciation. Such changes are easy to diagnose and relatively infrequent.

Third, *permanent* exogenous changes in the terms of trade may call for changes in competitiveness.[7] Terms of trade changes are again easy to observe, although judgment is certainly required to distinguish transitory from permanent changes. Even where changes are essentially permanent, as with the oil price increase of 1973, it does not necessarily follow that the real exchange rate should change greatly. Real exchange rate changes were called for to the extent that it was necessary to redistribute deficits among the oil importers, but they could not adjust away the surplus of the Organization of Petroleum Exporting Countries (OPEC), which depended only on the value of oil exports and the quantity of imports that OPEC chose to buy. In this instance the OPEC surplus changed underlying capital flows in a way that went a long way toward neutralizing the effect of changes in demand and supply.

This discussion suggests that, while fundamental equilibrium exchange rates are not immutable, they are not likely to change frequently and drastically. Moreover, it is possible to identify the factors that are likely to have a perceptible impact on (real) FEERs, and it is easy to trace the changes

---

6. This is true, at least, when real exchange rates are measured by a broadly based price index like the CPI or GDP deflator. See the classic analysis of Balassa (1964).

7. The terms of trade is defined as the price of exports *divided by* the price of imports, while competitiveness or the real exchange rate is measured by the price of home-produced tradable goods *divided by* the price of competing foreign products. The two concepts reduce to the same thing in the simple exportables-importables model of trade theory, but they are very different in the real world. Thus an oil price rise worsens the terms of trade of an oil-importing country, but need not influence its competitiveness. In general a large country's terms of trade are influenced *both* by exogenous factors like the real price of oil *and* by endogenous factors like its level of income and competitiveness.

in nominal rates required to maintain real rates constant in the presence of differential inflation. Nevertheless, unlike the market equilibrium rate, there is no simple objective test of whether or not a rate is in fundamental equilibrium. At best, estimates of the FEER require judgments that in practice contain subjective elements regarding cyclical adjustment, the underlying capital flow, and trade elasticities. At worst, skeptics deny any hope of identifying the fundamental equilibrium rate. It is certainly true that the concept has a normative element, inasmuch as what constitute the "underlying capital flow" and "internal balance" depend on the macroeconomic policy regarded as appropriate. But the scope for differences to arise from pure divergencies in value judgments should not be exaggerated: one can sensibly debate the size (and sometimes the sign) of the capital flows needed to maximize welfare, and how much scope there is for expanding demand without rekindling inflation. Views on these topics *are* modified in the light of new evidence, even though one never expects to achieve unanimity.

CURRENT EQUILIBRIUM   This term is intended to indicate the rate that would obtain if markets had full knowledge of all relevant facts and reacted rationally to that knowledge. The current equilibrium rate will depend upon such temporary factors as the path of interest rates, which in turn depends on the stance of macroeconomic policy and the state of the business cycle, and, given risk aversion, on net asset positions vis-à-vis the rest of the world. The current equilibrium rate will deviate from fundamental equilibrium when policy variables are set at levels which drive the exchange rate away from its FEER. For example, a high interest rate relative to other countries will appreciate the currency involved, so as to create expectations of a yield-equalizing depreciation over the period that the high interest rate is expected to persist, as in the classic Dornbusch (1976) analysis.

This is the concept of equilibrium that most economists have in mind when they model the behavior of exchange rates, and hence further understanding of the properties of the current equilibrium rate can be obtained by studying the voluminous professional literature on exchange rate determination. It is apparently also sometimes what is meant by "the rate justified by fundamentals"; clarity would be served if individuals who use this phrase would specify whether they are referring to the fundamental equilibrium rate or to the current equilibrium rate.

Given that knowledge is not perfect, one has to interpret the concept of the current equilibrium rate in a rational expectations sense, as the rate expected to equalize yields on comparable assets (in the simple case of risk neutrality) on the basis of currently available information. Like the market equilibrium rate, the current equilibrium rate adjusts in response to relevant news. It also refers to a nominal rather than a real rate. However, unlike the market equilibrium rate, identification of the current equilibrium rate requires subjective judgment.

The Size of Misalignments

Since a misalignment has been defined as a deviation of the market rate from fundamental equilibrium, measurement of the misalignment existing at any particular time requires an estimate of fundamental equilibrium. Such estimates are sought below. But before moving on to that task, one may observe that there is a second way of gaining a general idea of the size that misalignments have reached that does not depend on the credibility of any particular estimates of FEERs, but solely on the hypothesis that *changes* in those fundamental equilibrium rates have not been large.

Table 2 therefore shows the maximum swings in the real effective exchange rates[8] of the five major currencies for the decade since floating started in

TABLE 2   **Maximum swings in real effective exchange rates of five major currencies, 1963–72 and 1973–82** (percentages)

	1963–72	1973–82
Deutschemark	13	22
French franc	27	19
Japanese yen	14	35
Pound sterling	17	60
US dollar	14	32
Average	17	34

Note: The results presented in the table cannot be dismissed as a reflection of wild swings in the first couple of years after floating was adopted, when the market was still undergoing a learning process. Elimination of the period 1973–75 would alter the figures only for the DM and French franc, reducing them marginally to 18 percent and 17 percent, respectively. (Deletion of the years 1963–65 would have a rather similar effect, reducing the figures for the French franc and yen to 24 percent and 10 percent, respectively.)
Source: IMF statistics for relative wholesale prices vis-à-vis other industrial countries.

----

8. As measured by the IMF index of relative wholesale prices. The behavior of this index for the three major countries can be compared with that of 9 other indices of real effective exchange rates in appendix figures A1–A3.

1973 to the end of 1982. For comparability, figures are also provided for a similar 10-year period immediately prior to the abandonment of the adjustable peg and covering the breakdown of the Bretton Woods system. It is natural to present such estimates in terms of "real"—i.e., inflation-adjusted— exchange rates when seeking to measure misalignments, since differential inflation changes the equilibrium position measured in nominal terms. Similarly, it is natural to use "effective"—i.e., average (trade-weighted)— exchange rates, so as to avoid the equilibrium position's varying with changes in exchange rates among other currencies. There are various different measures of real effective exchange rates, which differ in the price indices they employ to adjust for inflation (wholesale prices in manufacturing, unit labor costs, consumer prices, etc.) and in the weights they use to compare different competitors (bilateral trade weights, bilateral weights modified to account for competition in third markets, multilateral weights based on comparative GNP or on the competitive relations implied by the IMF's multilateral exchange rate model, etc.). Appendix figures A1–A3 compare a number of such measures for the three major currencies. It is apparent that the different indices generally tell much the same story, although divergencies can be sufficiently large to preclude attributing significance to movements less than 5 percent or so. (Different measures can drift apart over time by considerably more than this, but a change of 5 percent is rarely accompanied by an *opposite* movement of another index in the short run.) For purposes of the exercises reported below, six of the leading indices were combined into a composite index.[9] The behavior of these composite indices for the five major countries is shown in appendix figure A4.

Table 2 reveals that for four of the five currencies the maximum swings in real effective exchange rates (REERs) have been greater in the decade of floating than they were in the previous decade. Indeed, on average swings were twice as large under floating. There was, however, one currency (the French franc) for which the swing was actually less, and another (the DM) for which the swing much less than doubled. It is worth noting that those two currencies are the two that participated in the European Monetary System (and its predecessor, the snake), which has meant that a large part of the

---

9. The composite indices are geometric means of the following series: *wholesale price indices—* Bank for International Settlements (BIS), Morgan Guaranty, IMF (63 ey 110); *unit labor costs—* BIS, IMF (65 um 110), IMF (65 umc 110). The French computation excludes the BIS-WPI series, which inexplicably moves far out of line with all others.

trade of Germany and, for much of the period, of France, has been conducted across pegged exchanges. Moreover, those pegs were periodically changed, in a way that roughly offset differential inflation.

The swings in the real effective exchange rates of the three independently floating currencies have, however, been enormous: in every case they have exceeded 30 percent. Moreover, as illustrated for the dollar and the pound in appendix figures A5 and A6, the nominal exchange rate swings have often exaggerated rather than offset the changes in competitiveness resulting from differential inflation.

If the fundamental equilibrium exchange rate were constant over time, then one could infer that the US dollar (for example) *must* have been misaligned at some time since 1973 by *at least* 16 percent (one-half of 32 percent). If the FEER were not exactly halfway between the highest and lowest values that the dollar touched, then misalignment must at some time have been even *greater* than 16 percent. Misalignments may admittedly have been smaller, to the extent that exchange rate changes were reflecting changes in fundamental equilibrium rates. But this analysis leaves a presumption that misalignments have been very substantial under floating, contrary to the expectation that was prevalent when floating rates were first accepted in 1973.

The Identification of Fundamental Equilibrium Rates

The traditional approach to estimating fundamental equilibrium exchange rates involves seeking a period during which exchange rates appear to have been at appropriate levels, and then making a "purchasing power parity" (PPP) comparison to identify the nominal exchange rate that would reproduce the real exchange rate of the base period *given* intervening inflation. For example, if the domestic country has suffered on average 10 percent more inflation than its trading partners since the base date, then one concludes that its currency should have depreciated by 10 percent compared to that base level. If instead the currency had appreciated by 5 percent in effective terms, then one would judge that the currency was 15 percent overvalued (in terms of the real effective exchange rate) compared to its fundamental equilibrium level.

An important technical issue concerns the choice of a price index for use in making PPP comparisons. Ideally one wants a measure that is *able* to diverge—as wholesale prices of primary products are not, under conditions

TABLE 3   **Real effective exchange rates relative to "equilibrium" base**
(index numbers, base period = 100)

Source	Base period	Date	US dollar
Morgan Guaranty[a]	March 1973	1977	100.0
Morgan Guaranty[a]	March 1973	1982	116.9
Morgan Guaranty[a]	March 1973	1983 Q1	117.0
Morgan Guaranty[b]	1980–82	1977	93.9
Morgan Guaranty[b]	1980–82	1982	109.8
Morgan Guaranty[b]	1980–82	1983 Q1	110.2
CEA	1973–80	1977	101.4
CEA	1973–80	1982	121.7

CEA Council of Economic Advisers.
Note: A number greater than 100 signifies a currency appreciated above its base value.
Sources: Morgan Guaranty, *World Financial Markets,* July and August 1983; Council of Economic Advisers' *Annual Report,* 1983, ch. 3 and table B-100.
a. Old series.
b. New series.

of efficient arbitrage; but that diverges *only* as the competitive position of the tradable sector changes—and not because (for example) consumer prices rise relative to the prices of tradables as a result of rapid productivity growth in the latter sector. The first criterion rules out export prices and argues for the use of wholesale prices of manufacturing *output* rather than *inputs*. The second criterion argues against the use of consumer prices.[10] Another choice relates to the use of an index of prices, which runs the danger that it may fail to reveal a deterioration in competitive position when suppliers shave their profit margins to defend their market share, versus an index of costs, which has the disadvantage that its coverage is usually only partial (specifically, that it is normally restricted to labor costs and excludes capital costs—though the IMF does publish a series based on value-added deflators which attempts to remedy this problem). There does not seem any convincing

10. An additional argument against the use of consumer prices applies where the price index is to be employed as the basis of a PPP rule for adjusting the exchange rate. This stems from the fact that what could be a purely transitory rise in consumer prices—for example, as a result of a bad harvest—would get built into the inflationary process if it were allowed to result in a depreciation.

Japanese yen	Deutschemark	French franc	Pound sterling
93.5	102.5	96.1	101.6
82.8	96.4	95.6	135.2
88.8	97.7	95.7	124.3
103.7	105.4	99.8	73.8
92.3	99.1	97.7	98.8
96.9	100.6	97.9	90.6

reason for preferring one type of index to the other, which is why the composite index used in this study (see footnote 9) combines indices using both wholesale prices and unit labor costs.

Table 3 shows some existing estimates of real effective exchange rates of the five major currencies based on the traditional PPP approach. The first three rows show the figures that Morgan Guaranty was using until July 1983, which employed March 1973 as a base when exchange rates were supposedly in equilibrium. The next three rows present the figures that Morgan Guaranty now uses, which have been rebased to take 1980–82 as a base. This naturally has the effect of cutting the measured overvaluation of those currencies that experienced a large real appreciation between March 1973 and 1980–82, namely the US dollar and even more so the pound sterling. The final rows present the effective real overvaluation of the US dollar implicit in the choice of 1973–80 as a base and the use of the Federal Reserve Board's index of real effective exchange rates, as was done by the US Council of Economic Advisers in its 1983 *Annual Report*.

There are two obvious deficiencies in the procedure whose results are shown in table 3. The first is that any base date chosen is bound to be somewhat arbitrary: there never was a golden age to which one can look back when the world economy was in general equilibrium. This criticism can be met to some extent, though not totally, by taking as the base the average real effective exchange rate over some lengthy period, rather than its value on a specific date. The second deficiency is that the procedure makes no allowance for any change in the FEER that may have occurred since the base period in order to accommodate to changed circumstances. There *are* events which call for changes in the real effective exchange rate in order to promote adjustment: for example, permanent shifts in the terms of trade which have to be offset, and changes in the balance between thrift and productivity which make it rational to accept a larger or smaller surplus or deficit on the current account of the balance of payments. These deficiencies are glaringly apparent in the large changes in measured competitive positions that have resulted from Morgan Guaranty's recent decision to rebase its series: one may enthusiastically agree that a March 1973 base is outmoded (because of the second deficiency), while remaining utterly unconvinced that the choice of a 1980–82 base addresses the first deficiency.

The present treatment seeks to remedy both those deficiencies in the traditional approach. Rather than search for a specific date or period when it may plausibly be argued that exchange rates were in equilibrium, it asks: what set of exchange rates would have been needed in a specific period, for which 1976–77 was chosen, to induce a set of current account balances that matched "underlying capital flows"? And in addition to extrapolating the exchange rates calculated to have represented "fundamental equilibrium" for 1976–77 forward by a mechanistic application of PPP, it asks what real changes in the interim have been sufficiently large to have had a macroeconomic impact, and seeks to make appropriate allowances. The assumptions needed to carry out such an exercise are undoubtedly heroic. The justification for nonetheless undertaking the exercise is that it is much less arbitrary than crude PPP extrapolations.

Underlying Capital Flows

A first step in estimating the FEERs for 1976–77 is to derive estimates for what have been called the "underlying capital flows" reflecting "thrift and productivity." It is easy enough to accept such a notion in concept. One expects that during any short time period the actual inflow or outflow of capital recorded by a country will reflect many short-term factors of a volatile nature: confidence, monetary policies relative to those abroad, speculation, timing accidents, and so on. At one time it was assumed that most such volatile movements would involve transactions in short-term assets, and conversely that the underlying capital flow could be approximated by transactions in assets with a long term to maturity. Unfortunately for analytical simplicity, neither assumption seems a reasonable approximation any more: many volatile flows involve switching into or out of long-term assets, while accumulation of working balances placed in short-term assets can be rather stable in aggregate. But this statistical difficulty in distinguishing volatile from underlying capital movements does not render the distinction unnecessary, for over a longer time horizon the short-term factors will tend to balance out, and what remains will be a reflection of the savings-investment balance in the economy. A country with a high rate of investment (in reflection of a high productivity of capital) relative to the level of domestically generated savings will find it advantageous to import capital (although the extent to which it is able to do so may be constrained by creditworthiness considerations). Conversely, a country with a high net savings rate and relatively few current investment opportunities can benefit by using a part of its savings to acquire investments abroad.

Unless public policy is distorting the level of saving (or conceivably investment) in a major way, the inflow or outflow of capital that results from such considerations will normally be socially beneficial, whether by augmenting domestic savings to permit a higher level of investment to be sustained, or by allowing savings to be invested in a more productive way (abroad). But realization of that potential gain requires that the capital flow be matched by a corresponding transfer of real resources. That is, it requires a matching current account surplus or deficit, so that the overall balance of payments is in equilibrium. Thus current account targets are the mirror image of underlying capital flows.

Problems arise when trying to translate these uncontroversial general principles into hard figures, given that the term to maturity is a poor indicator of volatility so that basic balance equilibrium is not a satisfactory target. We do not have the data on time preferences and marginal efficiencies of investment that might in principle allow welfare-maximizing capital flows to be estimated. But it would also be silly to pretend that we cannot develop any estimates as to the order of magnitude of desirable capital flows.

When I lived in Brazil in the late 1970s, I used to argue that an appropriate current account target for Brazil would be a deficit of about $5 billion a year. Critics objected to the propriety of discussing such targets, and then proceeded to debate whether the figure should not have been $4 billion or $6 billion, but no one ever told me that a country with such promising prospects as Brazil should *not* have been importing capital on a substantial scale to accelerate its development nor that the proper target would have been over $9 billion a year (the actual average level of foreign borrowing from 1977 to 1981, which led to disaster).

Getting a reasonable idea of the ''underlying'' or desirable capital flow is even more difficult for the five major countries than for Brazil. A natural starting point is to consider the actual average current account outcome over a reasonably lengthy period: the average balance over the 1974–78 cycle is shown in the first row of table 4. It can be seen that the United States was in balance, that Germany and Japan were in large surplus, while France and the United Kingdom were in substantial deficit. Another approach is to look at long-term capital outflows, despite their inadequacies as noted above. The second row of table 4 reveals that for the four countries other than the United States the capital flows were broadly consistent with the state of their current balances. The United States, however, had a vast capital outflow without a corresponding current account surplus. The question therefore arises as to whether the capital outflow was a reflection of thrift and productivity which did not lead to a real transfer because of flawed adjustment policies, or whether the current account outcome was more consistent with the investment-savings balance while the capital outflow reflected lax monetary policies permitted by the dollar's reserve role.

Some data relevant to answering that question are shown in table 5. What stands out from this table is the low savings rate in the United States. Although the United States probably still has the highest capital-labor ratio in the world, it would seem impossible to argue that the discrepancy is so great that the United States would be justified in transferring a significant

TABLE 4   **Data relevant to assessing underlying capital flows**
(billion dollars, 1977 prices)

	United States	Japan	Germany	France	United Kingdom	Total
Actual current account balance, 1974–78 average	0.1	4.8	5.8	−2.7	−3.0	5.0
Long-term net capital outflow, 1974–78 average	13.7	4.2	3.6	−0.7	−3.2	17.6

Note: Figures adjusted to 1977 prices by US wholesale price index.
Sources: OECD *Economic Outlook,* IMF *International Financial Statistics.*

TABLE 5   **Savings and investment in five major countries, 1976–77**
(percentage of GDP, average of 1976 and 1977)

	United States	Japan	Germany	France	United Kingdom
Savings					
Household	4.2	16.2	8.4	9.5	4.6
Corporate	1.6	1.0	1.4	−0.4	2.6
Government	−1.0	2.2	1.8	2.2	−0.7
Total	4.7	19.4	11.5	11.3	6.5
Net investment					
Household	2.7	6.5	8.0	5.4	0.9
Corporate	1.5	7.2		4.8	5.1
Government	1.5	4.9	2.7	2.2	2.6
Total	5.6	18.6	10.7	12.4	8.6
Current account	−0.5	1.2	0.9	−1.1	−1.1
Statistical discrepancy	−0.4	−0.4	0.0	0.0	−1.1

Note: Totals may not add due to rounding.
Source: OECD National Accounts.

proportion of its limited savings overseas. A balanced current account seems a more reasonable objective. France was at that time the fastest growing economy of the five apart from high-savings Japan, so its role as a capital importer was appropriate. The United Kingdom was in the mid-1970s investing heavily in capital-intensive North Sea oil development, so it was again quite rational to be importing capital. The position of Japan and Germany as capital exporters seems perfectly consistent with their savings-investment balances.

The remaining question is how large the capital imports by France and the United Kingdom and the capital exports by Japan and Germany should ideally have been. In order to apply the IMF's multilateral exchange rate model (MERM) and to limit the specification of current account objectives to the big five, the sum of the objectives must equal the sum of the actual outcomes of the five.[11] That sum averaged $1.4 billion in 1976–77. In view of the

11. One reason this exercise has been performed on a past period rather than on current data is to exploit this knowledge. In working out such targets for future application, it would be important that the interests of the rest of the world be introduced into the decision making of the five.

difficulties that both the United Kingdom and France experienced in financing their current account deficits at times in the mid-1970s, it seems clear that their actual deficits of around $3 billion a year were too large. A figure of around half that would represent my best judgment of what a reasonable target would have been. If one assumes that Japan and Germany should have had equal targets, arithmetic dictates that those targets would have been something over $2 billion a year.

The current account targets (or underlying capital outflows) suggested as reasonable by the preceding discussion are shown in the second column of table 6. As with the Brazilian target mentioned above, it would be silly to argue about their last billion dollars, but, at least to the writer, there seem to be quite strong arguments against figures drastically different from those in the table.

Estimates of FEERs in 1976–77

Apart from nonprice competitiveness, which is nonquantifiable and in any event is unlikely to change rapidly, there are three factors that have a major systematic impact on the current account. The first is the terms of trade (see footnote 7). The second is the relative pressure of demand at home as against that in foreign markets. The third is price competitiveness, measured by the real effective exchange rate. Algebraically, one may write:

$$\begin{matrix} \text{Current} \\ \text{balance} \end{matrix} = f\left\{ \begin{matrix} \text{terms of} \\ \text{trade} \end{matrix}; \begin{matrix} \text{relative pressure} \\ \text{of demand} \end{matrix}; \text{REER} \right\}.$$

TABLE 6   **Current account balances, targets, and desired changes, 1976–77**
(billion dollars, 1977 prices)

	Actual current balance	Target current balance	Desirable change in current account balance
United States	−4.7	0	+4.7
Japan	7.4	2.2	−5.2
Germany	4.2	2.2	−2.0
France	−4.6	−1.5	+3.1
United Kingdom	−0.9	−1.5	−0.6
Total	1.4	1.4	0.0

Sources: OECD *Economic Outlook* and reasoning described in text.

Since the terms of trade are partly influenced by factors exogenous to individual countries (like the real price of oil) and partly by relative demand pressures and REERs, as explained in footnote 7, this equation can in principle be solved for that value of the REER needed to produce a given current balance when relative demand pressures are cyclically normal. It is this value of the REER that has been defined as the FEER—a concept that is, as argued above, itself defined in terms of the REER. (It might have been more accurate to speak of a fundamental equilibrium real effective exchange rate, or FEREER, but there are limits to the extent to which authors can abuse their readers with inelegant acronyms!)

The question therefore arises as to whether relative demand pressures were cyclically normal in the period 1976–77 chosen as the base for this exercise. Unfortunately there do not now seem to be any published estimates of GNP gaps on an internationally comparable basis. The best figures to assess relative demand pressures would therefore seem to be the unemployment statistics, standardized for international comparability, published by the Organization for Economic Cooperation and Development (OECD). Unemployment is, however, a lagging indicator of the pressure of demand, so that demand pressures in 1976–77 are best measured by the unemployment levels of 1977, as shown in table 7. Column 4 then shows the excess of 1977 unemployment over the country's average for the 1974–79 cycle. The final column compares that excess with the excess for the OECD as a whole, to get an indicator of whether demand in each country was cyclically more or less slack than abroad.

It appears that most countries were fairly close to the cyclical average at

TABLE 7   **Unemployment as a measure of 1976–77 demand pressure in five major countries** (percentages)

	Average 1974–79	1976	1977	Excess of 1977 over cyclical average	Excess of country excess over OECD
United States	6.6	7.5	6.9	0.3	−0.1
Japan	1.9	2.0	2.0	0.1	−0.3
Germany	3.2	3.7	3.7	0.5	0.1
France	4.5	4.4	4.7	0.2	−0.2
United Kingdom	5.1	5.5	6.2	1.1	0.7
OECD	4.9	5.2	5.3	0.4	0.0

Source: OECD *Main Economic Indicators.*

that time. (The suspicion that this would be so in fact led to the choice of 1976–77 as the base period for these calculations.) The United Kingdom is an exception, which, according to this measure, had slacker demand than the other countries. In view of the United Kingdom's failure to master inflation in this period, however, it would seem difficult to argue that Britain was suffering from an abnormally high level of unnecessary slack in 1976–77. There is also some question as to whether an adjustment might be in order for the United States, where unemployment was falling rapidly, in contrast to the other countries. Such an adjustment would reduce the underlying US deficit below the measured deficit, and would therefore appreciate the estimated dollar FEER, somewhat. In the end, however, no adjustments were made for abnormal cyclical positions.

This means that the desired changes in current account balances (shown in the last column of table 6) can be found simply by subtracting the actual current balance (column 1) from the target (in column 2). How much would exchange rates have had to adjust in order to produce those changes in current balances, after lag effects had worked themselves out? There is one model, the IMF's multilateral exchange rate model (MERM), that was built with the precise object of answering that type of question. The version presented in Artus and McGuirk (1981) is based on 1977 data and can therefore be applied directly. It yields answers in the form of changes in bilateral nominal exchange rates against the dollar, which are shown in the first column of table 8. These numbers then have to be transformed into effective exchange rates, which can be done by applying the MERM weights. Since the MERM allows for the partial neutralization of exchange rate changes through induced internal

TABLE 8   **Exchange rate changes needed to achieve fundamental equilibrium, 1976–77** (percentages)

	Bilateral dollar exchange rate	EER	REER
United States	n.a.	−4.9	−4.2
Japan	11.9	10.2	8.8
Germany	6.5	3.9	3.0
France	−2.9	−7.1	−5.5
United Kingdom	6.9	3.4	2.1
Other industrial countries	2.9	−0.8	−0.6

n.a. Not applicable.
Sources: Table 6 and the MERM (Artus and McGuirk, 1981).

inflation, the implicit changes in *real* effective exchange rates are smaller than the needed changes in effective exchange rates calculated by the MERM. How much smaller they are can be estimated from the MERM's predictions of the effect of a 10 percent depreciation of a country's own currency on its GDP deflator. For example, the version of the MERM used for the present simulation, the version with "low-feedback parameters," implies that a 10 percent nominal depreciation of the French franc would raise French prices by 2.3 percent (Artus and McGuirk, 1981, table 2, p. 296), which—abstracting from any difference between the GDP deflator and the price indices used to measure real exchange rates—implies a real depreciation of 7.7 percent. Applying such "offset coefficients" to the effective exchange rate (EER) changes in the second column of table 8 yields the REER changes shown in the final column.

The MERM calculates only the *change* in exchange rates needed to achieve a specified *change* in current balances. To derive from this the *level* of the FEER, one needs to know the actual level of the exchange rate. Unfortunately the appropriate rate to take as the "actual" is not unambiguous, due to the well-established fact that exchange rate changes affect trade flows with lengthy distributed lags. For example, the MERM is supposed to show the changes that would occur after a lag of two to three years. Clearly the *average* lag is less than that, perhaps of the order of six months to a year. Hence one should calculate the FEERs for 1976–77 by applying the adjustments shown in the last column of table 8 to the average REERs for 1975–76, as is done in the last two columns of table 9. However, earlier columns show data on REERs for individual years in the period 1974–77,

TABLE 9   **Actual REERs and estimated FEERs for 1976–77**
(index numbers, 1975 = 100)

	REERs					FEERS
	1974	1975	1976	1977	1975–76 av.	1976–77
United States	102.8	100	103.6	101.5	101.8	98
Japan	108.6	100	101.2	106.4	100.6	109
Germany	106.1	100	100.2	103.5	100.1	103
France	89.9	100	98.1	93.4	99.0	94
United Kingdom	93.9	100	92.7	94.2	96.4	98

Sources: Composite data on REERs from appendix and table 8.

to allow those who would prefer a different base to see how much difference it would make.

Appendix figures A4 and A7–A11 use the FEERs presented in table 9 as a base from which to display the variation of REERs over time. The arguments used to derive the FEERs have been presented in sufficient detail that those who question particular assumptions should be able to estimate roughly how much difference their preferred assumptions would make in the results, and thus assess whether their disagreements would produce changes that are large relative to the actual variations of exchange rates in the decade since floating commenced.

Extrapolating FEERs to 1983

In order to assess the size of present misalignments, it is necessary to consider how much FEERs may have changed since 1976–77. There would seem to have been three new developments in that period potentially important enough to have exerted a perceptible impact on the FEERs of one or more of the major powers: the second oil price increase, the coming on stream of North Sea oil (for the United Kingdom), and the emergence of the United States as a large net capital importer.

If the 1979–80 oil price increase is judged to be permanent, it implies a need for (real) exchange rate adjustments to the extent that there is a differential payments impact on different industrial countries that should be

TABLE 10   **Changes in REERs needed to neutralize trade balance effects of oil price increases** (percentages)

	Change in oil price from			
	1972–78	*1972–80*	*1978–80*	*1978–83*
United States	0	4	4	2
Japan	− 11	− 28	− 15	− 8
Germany	0	− 3	− 3	− 2
France	− 1	− 3	− 2	− 1
United Kingdom	12	23	10	6

Source: McGuirk (1983, table 12).

adjusted away rather than absorbed by offsetting changes in savings or investment. It is convenient to assume that adjustments to the oil price increase will be complete by 1985, so that by then OPEC will be spending all its additional income while energy demand and supply in the industrial countries will have adjusted to the new oil price level. (In 1983 OPEC is in fact in current account deficit, but it is questionable whether this will be sustained in the medium term with a constant oil price: creditworthiness constraints will limit the deficits that the ''high absorbers'' can afford, while the ''low absorbers'' will surely move back into surplus, to an extent that makes the assumption of overall OPEC balance reasonable.) Assuming that changes in OPEC import demand are distributed proportionately among the industrial countries, this permits calculation of incipient current account imbalances. McGuirk (1983) used the MERM to calculate the changes in REERs needed to restore current balance. Table 10 shows her estimates in the first two columns: the third is derived as the difference between the first two. The fourth reflects the erosion in the real price of oil from 1980 to 1983.

It is evident that the needed changes are quite modest, except in the two extreme cases of Japan (which is exceptionally dependent on oil imports) and the United Kingdom (which is a net oil exporter). They would be even more modest if a judgment were made that the oil price was likely to fall further. Another possible offsetting factor of relevance to the United Kingdom is the limited life of the oil fields whose current production is responsible for the sterling appreciation shown in table 10: if one takes the view that a part of the increased real income resulting from North Sea oil should be saved in the form of an increased current surplus, the justified appreciation would be smaller than calculated by McGuirk.

The second relevant development since 1977 is the change in the status of the United Kingdom from major oil importer to significant oil exporter. (The United Kingdom is currently the world's fifth largest oil producer, and oil exports account for over a fifth of total exports.) It has been calculated that, given the limited expected production lifetime of the North Sea oil fields, rational utilization of the income from North Sea oil would require saving about one-half of the oil revenue (Forsyth and Kay, 1980). Since investment in a country like the United Kingdom is primarily constrained by interest rates and expected real wages adjusted for productivity rather than by the availability of savings, that additional saving should be reflected largely in an increased surplus in the current account of the balance of payments. Anne McGuirk's estimate in column 2 of table 10, adjusted downward to allow for the erosion in the real oil price since 1980, would suggest that a real sterling appreciation of about 17 percent would have been needed to adjust away the whole of the oil surplus. If one takes the view that a half of the oil bonanza should have been saved, the desirable appreciation is halved to, say, 9 percent. This is *inclusive* of the sterling appreciation shown in the last column of table 10, not additional.

The most difficult question is whether the emergence of a structural budget deficit in the United States should lead to a revision of the dollar's FEER. Given the large tax cuts and the increases in defense spending not matched by equivalent reductions in other forms of government spending, it looks as if the United States will be running massive budget deficits in the next few years. This will reduce aggregate net US savings, by a similar order of magnitude that the first oil price increase raised world savings in the mid-1970s.[12] Feldstein (1983a) has argued that, while the deficit itself should be regretted, the second-best response to the deficit involves high real interest rates, capital imports, a high value of the dollar, and a current account deficit. If one accepts the US budget deficit as exogenous, one can scarcely reject the "Feldstein doctrine," and that would imply adjusting the FEER to reflect the fall in US thrift so as to allow the United States to borrow from the rest of the world.

But two further questions must be asked before one accepts the logic of the Feldstein doctrine. The first is whether the economic strategy of budget deficit, high real interest rates, foreign borrowing, overvalued currency, and current account deficit is *sustainable*. This is, after all, qualitatively similar to the policy package that evolved under President Lopez Portillo in Mexico (although the scale of the borrowing relative to GNP is perhaps only a third as large). Until 1982 the market was happily financing what everyone now recognizes to have been an unsustainable policy course in Mexico. The mere fact that the market is equally happily bidding the dollar up to new highs as

---

12. The tax cuts are estimated to have reduced revenue by about 4 percent of US GNP or $120 billion, and thus to have reduced total US savings by the order of $100 billion. OPEC ran a current surplus on the order of $40 billion per annum in the mid-1970s, equivalent to a rise in savings *ex ante* of perhaps $50 billion per annum. US prices have increased about 75 percent since 1975.

this is written does not prove that current US policy is on a sustainable course: if confidence collapses, the result may be very unpleasant indeed.

While such a collapse seems likely (at some date) on present policies, it would be rash to assert that it is inevitable: a gradual return to fiscal responsibility might permit a "soft landing." But even if one is optimistic on that score, one has a second question to consider: whether large-scale net borrowing by the most capital-rich country on earth to enable it temporarily to lower its savings rate is really economically rational? With all due respect to the desirability of economists' exhibiting a decent humility, we surely have a rather strong hunch on the answer to that question.

One has to conclude that it would be quite wrong to accept macroeconomic follies like the US budget deficit as exogenous, and accommodate them without further question (by adjusting the FEER). On the contrary, a principal purpose of seeking a more structured exchange rate system is precisely to expose such examples of myopic and internationally inconsistent national decision making. If the administration had to explain that its budgetary policy required approval of an appreciation of the dollar's FEER, which Congress could recognize would threaten a large number of tradable goods industries, it is surely likely that political forces to restore fiscal discipline would be strengthened. To rationalize recent exchange rates and argue for automatic adjustment of the FEER to reflect the budget deficit would gut this potentially important political force, as well as imply agreement that policy is on a sustainable and satisfactory course. Accordingly, no adjustment to the dollar's FEER has been made on this score.

There is, however, a second recent development that might justify some change in the underlying capital inflow of the United States: namely, the swing of direct investment from a normal net outflow of around $8 billion a year to an average inflow in the last two years of over $12 billion. Even if the recent figures prove erratically high, it seems reasonable to allow for a swing of say $12 billion. Using the customary rule of thumb that each 1 percent dollar depreciation improves the current account balance by about $3 billion a year, this suggests that a real appreciation of 4 percent might be justified on this score.

In addition to the discrete events considered above, continuing differences in productivity trends may call for changes in measured real exchange rates to maintain competitiveness constant. This would certainly be true if the indices underlying the composite included CPIs. With indices based on WPIs and unit labor costs, the only country for which such an adjustment seems called for is Japan. If the behavior of the index of export prices relative to

TABLE 11 **Estimates of misalignments, 1983 Q1**

	Actual REER (1976–77 FEER = 100)	Changes in FEERs 1977–83 (percentage)	Effective exchange rate relative to estimated fundamental equilibrium[a]	Fundamental equilibrium rate against US dollar	Nominal appreciation needed against US dollar (percentage)
US dollar	122.9	+6	116	n.a.	n.a.
Japanese yen	89.6	−2	91	¥ 205	15
Deutschemark	92.7	−2	95	DM 1.98	22
French franc	96.6	−1	98	FF 5.79	19
Pound sterling	118.4	+9	109	$ 1.64	7
Other industrial country currencies	n.a.	n.a.	98[b]	n.a.	16[c]

n.a. Not applicable.
Sources: Appendix table A1 and calculations described in text.
a. Actual REER with 1983 Q1 FEER = 100.
b. Residual.
c. Unweighted mean.

that of wholesale prices from 1976 to 1982 in Japan is compared with that in Germany (the only other major country that publishes an export price index), one finds that export prices fell 15 percent relative to wholesale prices in Japan and only 6 percent in Germany. Thus it seems that technical advances continue to be made with particular rapidity in Japan's tradable goods industries. To compensate for this, it was assumed that Japan's FEER as measured by the composite index appreciates at a rate of 1 percent a year. Accordingly the net depreciation of the yen's FEER was reduced, from the 8 percent shown in table 10, to 2 percent.

Current Misalignments

The real effective exchange rates of the five major currencies in the first quarter of 1983, the most recent period for which full data on REERs were available, are shown in the first column of table 11, using the estimated 1976–77 FEERs as a base. It can be seen, for example, that the dollar had appreciated in real effective terms by some 23 percent above the level that was previously calculated to have represented a fundamental equilibrium in the earlier period. The next column shows the real effective appreciation (+) or depreciation (−) that the previous section suggests would have been merited on the basis of changes in FEERs. For example, the oil price rise would have justified a real dollar appreciation of about 2 percent and the swing in direct investment a further 4 percent. Thus the estimate of dollar overvaluation is reduced somewhat, to 16 percent, as shown in column 3. That column also shows the pound to have been overvalued, while the yen, DM, and French franc were somewhat undervalued.

One can compare the misalignments estimated in this study with the results of Morgan Guaranty's calculations shown in table 3. On the March 1973 base that Morgan Guaranty has employed until recently, the pattern of overvaluation is reduced somewhat, to 16 percent, as shown in column 3. in table 11, though Morgan showed the pound as substantially more overvalued and the yen as somewhat more undervalued. The differences are more marked when comparison is made with Morgan Guaranty's new base of 1980–82. This reduces the dollar overvaluation and yen undervaluation, puts the DM in equilibrium, and transforms the pound into an *undervalued* currency. This occurs because the new base period includes the years 1980–81 when, by almost unanimous consent, the pound was grossly overvalued. The United Kingdom's current account surplus has already diminished greatly despite Britain's having easily the highest unemployment rate of the five major countries and despite the strong case for Britain's aiming to run large current account surpluses during the present brief interlude of oil abundance: the explanation for this failure unquestionably lies in a continuing sterling overvaluation. There could scarcely be a more compelling example of the inadequacy of the conventional procedure of plucking rates from some base period and treating them as equilibria, and of the need instead to engage in the type of exercise presented above.

This is not to claim that those calculations are at all precise: on the contrary, the approach requires a belief that it is better to be roughly right than to be precise but irrelevant. The procedures employed are uncomfortably *ad hoc*.[13]

---

13. An attempt was made to run simulations on two of the large multicountry econometric models to ask what constant real effective exchange rates would have been needed over the period 1974–77 to generate the desired pattern of current account surpluses and deficits in 1976–77 while achieving target levels of income in each country. It proved surprisingly difficult to change the variables that such models treat as exogenous in order to produce simulations that satisfied the desired constraints, and so in the end only the MERM was employed in the calculations.

Numerous heroic assumptions are needed. There is no way of calculating formal confidence intervals indicating the range beyond which FEERs are unlikely to lie: it is quite easy to change the base periods and other necessary inputs in ways that can alter the results by 5 percent to 10 percent. Indeed, it would be disingenuous to deny that some selection of the inputs in order to produce results that reflect one's presuppositions about FEERs is bound to take place when undertaking this type of exercise. The need to tell a consistent and credible story nevertheless limits the possibility of simply rationalizing one's preconceptions. Furthermore, undertaking such exercises provides the opportunity of engaging in serious debate out of which differences in view about FEERs may be narrowed. It remains open to anyone to provide a counterexample, but it is my impression that, without making major changes in the substantive assumptions, one would be unlikely to generate estimates that are more than 10 percent or so different from those presented in table 11.

The crucial point is that even a margin of error of 10 percent implies that exchange rates have been (and continue to be) misaligned. This is illustrated in appendix figures A7–A11, which display movements in the composite REER indices of the five major currencies since 1976. It was assumed that the FEER adjusted steadily from its 1976–77 value to its 1983 (Q1) value. Lines have then been drawn 10 percent either side of the implicit FEER line, to show when exchange rates have moved outside the zone that one can feel reasonably confident contained the FEER. It can be seen that all three of the independently floating currencies have moved outside these zones, two of them on both sides. Even the DM and French franc have come close to the edge of these rather wide zones. There is no indication that misalignments are subsiding over time as experience with floating accumulates; if anything, the reverse is true.

The final step is to convert the estimates of current FEERs in real effective terms back into a set of dollar exchange rates consistent with fundamental equilibrium. This was done using the MERM weights and treating the collective FEER of the smaller industrial countries as a residual. The results are shown in the fourth column of table 11. They suggest that a correct alignment in the first quarter of 1983 would have valued a dollar at about DM 1.98, ¥ 205, and FF 5.79, while the pound would have been worth some $1.64 and the smaller currencies would on average have needed to appreciate some 2 percent in real effective terms.

3   The Case for Managed Exchange Rates

The case for managing the exchange rate rests on the costs imposed by volatility and misalignments: the measures developed in the previous section show that both have been large and, if anything, increasing under floating. This section therefore proceeds to examine the nature of the costs involved. Having concluded that the major problems are those posed by misalignments, it goes on to enquire into possible causes of misalignments and subsequently to ask what would be sacrificed in using monetary policy to limit misalignments. The case for a managed rather than free-floating exchange rate rests on the judgment that the costs of misalignments exceed the benefits of treating the exchange rate as a residual in policy determination.

Costs of Volatility

It has traditionally been argued that an increase in price uncertainty resulting from more volatile exchange rates would lead to a reduction in trade and other international transactions. There is no doubt that a great deal of intraday volatility leads to wider buy-sell spreads, and those higher exchange transaction costs presumably do something to curtail trade, but spreads are still so low that the effect is minimal. What is much more important is the possibility that uncertainty regarding the domestic currency value of receipts from foreign transactions may lead to a bias against foreign trade, perhaps accompanied by a bias toward increased direct foreign investment as a way of servicing foreign markets less exposed to the vagaries of volatile exchange rates. Economists have for some time been searching for such effects. Until recently no evidence had been presented that trade among the industrial countries had been hampered by exchange rate volatility (see Clark and Haulk, 1972; Makin, 1976; and Hooper and Kohlhagen, 1978), although there was some evidence that exchange rate uncertainty has inhibited the trade of developing countries (see Coes, 1981, on Brazil, and Diaz-Alejandro, 1976, pp. 66–69, on Colombia).[14] However, Cushman (1983) reports a

---

14. The main source of exchange rate uncertainty in the case of the developing countries in question was the erratic pegging practices of their governments rather than the erratic market movements of a floating rate, but the impact on the private sector is similar.

significant negative effect of volatility of the real exchange rate on the trade level of several industrial countries.

That it proved easier to find evidence of the negative effect of exchange rate volatility on the trade of developing countries than it did in the case of the developed countries should not occasion surprise. Where adequate forward markets exist, traders can cover forward and so limit the impact of exchange rate volatility when they find this troubling. (It is not true that exchange risk can be *eliminated* by the use of forward markets, since there are virtually always lags between the decision to sign a contract and the ability to cover forward, as well as uncertainties about the precise time when payment will be received; but the impact of volatility can certainly be *reduced* by forward covering.) By and large, there exist reasonable forward markets, at least for short maturities, among the currencies of the industrial countries, but not for the currencies of the developing countries.

It has been suggested that short-run volatility of exchange rates may do something to contribute to longer run misalignments (Shafer and Loopesko, 1983). It is also true that volatility between the currencies of the industrial countries complicates the task of economic management in the developing countries, since it confronts these countries with the need to choose between stabilizing their effective exchange rates (which minimizes macroeconomic shocks) and stabilizing their bilateral rate against a major trading currency (which minimizes the risk of traders, who need to invoice in a specific currency).[15] Furthermore, exchange rate volatility diverts considerable managerial talent to the commercially necessary but socially unproductive activity of covering not only trade risk but also balance-sheet positions (even on a quarterly basis). But for all that, exchange rate volatility is a nuisance rather than a major source of concern: if this were the *principal* drawback in present arrangements, it is doubtful whether it would be worth contemplating major changes.

Costs of Misalignments

The costs of misalignments have received surprisingly little analysis in the economics literature up to now, presumably because misalignments—as

---

15. See Williamson (1982).

opposed to volatility—have not traditionally been recognized as a likely consequence of floating. Indeed, Shafer and Loopesko (1983) list as the first of four principal claims advanced by advocates of floating a decade ago that:

Price-adjusted or real exchange rates would be maintained relatively constant by stabilizing speculation, and would change mainly in response to shifts or trends in the equilibrium terms of trade between economies.

In fact misalignments were not eliminated by floating; indeed, the measures of the previous section suggest that misalignments have been about as large under floating as they were in the breakdown stage of the Bretton Woods system, when the approach adopted above suggests they reached some 20 percent to 30 percent for both the dollar and yen.

Such efforts as have been made to identify the costs of misalignments have generally pointed to the costs to a particular country at a specific time: to the unemployment caused by overvaluation or the inflation resulting from undervaluation. (See, for example, the cover story in *Business Week,* 27 June 1983.) There is, however, something unsatisfactory in this approach, inasmuch as the unemployment in country A has two (at least partial) offsets— less unemployment in its trading partners, and less inflation for itself.[16] When the position of the country is reversed, as it presumably is sooner or later, the country will benefit from lower unemployment (though suffer from increased inflationary pressure). It is only insofar as this sequence leads to less satisfactory long-run performance than would be attainable with the exchange rate maintained at its fundamental equilibrium level that one is entitled to attribute the cost to misaligned exchange rates.

There would seem to be six distinguishable costs imposed by misaligned exchange rates. These need not all apply simultaneously: indeed, by their nature several of them are *alternatives*.

CONSUMPTION VARIATIONS   This cost was first analyzed by Hause (1966) and subsequently elaborated by Johnson (1966). Suppose, it was argued, a country maintains a pegged exchange rate at an overvalued level for a time. Then, to preserve full employment when confronted with the fall in export demand and the rise in imports consequential on overvaluation, it will have

---

16. Haberler (1983) reminds us forcibly of this offsetting benefit of an overvalued exchange rate.

to expand demand for nontradable goods by enough to absorb the resources released from the tradable goods industries. But expanding demand for nontradables (especially when the substitution effect is pushing consumers to buy relatively more tradables) involves increasing consumption above the long-run sustainable level.

The policy also involves an unsustainable trade deficit, so in due course a devaluation occurs adequate to generate a current account surplus to recoup the reserve loss that resulted from the preceding overvaluation. To release resources for the balance of payments, consumption has to be cut back (even *below* the long-run sustainable level). But there is much evidence that most people feel worse off if they are obliged to vary their consumption sharply from one period to the next, even if their *average* level of consumption is no lower. Indeed, the notion forms the basis for the "permanent income hypothesis" and "life-cycle hypothesis," both of which postulate that people save primarily to even out their consumption stream to match their long-run, rather than current, income, and which are generally accepted as containing an important element of truth. Thus the dissatisfaction resulting from alternation of splurge and austerity constitutes the welfare cost of living with misaligned exchange rates.

Harry Johnson actually termed this "the welfare cost of exchange rate stabilization," on the implicit premise that significant misalignments would occur only when governments pegged exchange rates at levels that become misaligned, e.g., through differential inflation. It is obvious, however, that the analysis applies to misalignments *per se,* no matter what their source. It applies as much to the cutback in consumption that Americans must expect some time in the future to compensate for the looming trade deficit (the counterpart to present budgetary profligacy) as it does to the austerity that Mexicans are currently suffering as a consequence of having pursued similar policies in the period 1978–82; the difference in exchange regimes is immaterial. But the previous section suggests that misalignments have probably been as large since the advent of floating as they were in the worst phase of Bretton Woods. Johnson's label for this cost is a graphic illustration of the fact that economists failed to foresee that floating rates might lead to the large misalignments that have occurred.

ADJUSTMENT COSTS   The cost discussed above presumes that resources can be shifted costlessly between industries producing tradable goods and those producing nontradables. In reality this is far from true. The labor and capital released from employment in the auto and steel industries in the United States as a result *inter alia* of dollar overvaluation cannot be redeployed costlessly into producing the missiles and running the video arcades that are the counterpart to the US budget deficit.

Such adjustments can undoubtedly occur in the long run (however much noneconomists are prone to doubt it). But the process of adjustment requires the retraining of labor and the construction of new capital equipment, both of which absorb real resources. One of the reasons that the concept of the equilibrium real exchange rate is defined in long-run terms, as the rate that would be expected to secure an appropriate current account balance over the cycle as a whole, is precisely because it makes no sense to incur the costs that would be involved in shuttling resources back and forth so as to maintain continuous payments balance.

In a recent paper, J. David Richardson (1982) describes as "divergence mistakes" the errors that firms make when resource-allocation decisions are based on misleading price signals, such as misaligned exchange rates. He argues:

Divergence mistakes are costly not only because of human aversion to risk, but also because temporary competitive imbalances can generate empty shelves and storage lots in one location, excessive inventories in another, and resource-diverting arbitrage that transfers goods from the latter location to the former. The three respective resource allocational costs associated with divergence mistakes are waste from rationing, waste from excessive stockpiles, and waste from unnecessary transportation and redistribution.

Adjustment costs have received a certain amount of attention in the trade literature, in the context of the dislocation costs involved in liberalizing trade. The general conclusion (e.g. Magee, 1972) seems to be that such costs are significant, though well worth incurring in order to effect a permanent improvement in the allocation of resources. Obviously the cost-benefit comparison would look very different if the costs were accepted not in order to achieve an allocational improvement, but rather in response to temporary (and thus misleading) price signals.

UNEMPLOYMENT   The discussion up to now has supposed that full employment is maintained when an overvaluation develops. But in fact a major reason that adjustment is costly is that it does not start instantaneously. In the first instance, the labor and capital released from US tradable-goods industries as a result of dollar overvaluation simply remain unemployed, running to waste. The process of retraining typically starts only after months and years of unemployment, while capital redeployment is usually possible only as capital depreciates. Indeed, because of the costs of redeploying resources between sectors, it makes sense to undertake such adjustment only if there is an expectation that the shift in demand will be long-lasting.

Where it is expected that an overvaluation will prove temporary, unemployment in the tradable goods industries is a rational response to misalignment. Whether it is also socially optimal depends on how temporary the misalignment turns out to be. One of the problems of unstructured floating is that it leaves every agent to make his own inexpert judgment as to whether a change in the exchange rate represents a signal that should influence resource allocation or a temporary blip that should be ignored. In consequence it may well be that a change in the real exchange rate that is needed to effect adjustment is initially largely ignored, leading to larger unemployment costs than are necessary.

PRODUCTIVE CAPACITY   In an uncertain world, firms cannot be sure when an overvaluation is sufficiently temporary to merit adjustment rather than a decision to ride out the period of slack demand. An overvalued exchange rate may therefore induce a firm to scrap capacity that could be productively employed at equilibrium prices. Similarly, multinationals may shift new investment overseas and come to rely on foreign sources of supply. Even if a firm is convinced that it is worth maintaining its capacity until the misalignment is corrected, its creditors may not be so convinced. Firms that would be viable on the basis of equilibrium relative prices may be forced into bankruptcy, and capacity may again be destroyed inappropriately in the process. Recent experience in both the United States and Britain suggests that these dangers of an erosion of the industrial base, or ''deindustrialization,'' are all too real.

Analogous effects in overstimulating investment in the tradable goods sector may occur during a prolonged period of undervaluation, as arguably occurred in Germany and Japan in the 1960s. When the misalignment is corrected, the excessive investment will prove to have been unjustified and will have to be abandoned (or subsidized). If repeated misalignments give rise to great uncertainty about the equilibrium level of competitiveness, one might expect investment to be discouraged even though the exchange rate was not on average either overvalued or undervalued.

RATCHET EFFECTS ON INFLATION   It has often been hypothesized that a sequence of overvaluations and undervaluations tends to ratchet up the price level more than would occur with the maintenance of a similar pressure of demand and a constant real exchange rate. It is observed that depreciation produces strong inflationary pressures; as prices of imported inputs and consumer goods rise in consequence of depreciation, the prices of domestically produced goods are pulled up too, and trade unions seek (and are in a strong position to obtain) wage rises needed to prevent an erosion of living standards. Appreciation, it is argued, does not induce equivalent pressures to cut domestic prices and wages.

This is not to argue that a combination of weak demand and overvaluation does not contribute to restraint in wage demands (witness the recent United Auto Workers "givebacks"), but merely that the restraint is weaker than the pressure for wage increases in the opposite situation. Consequently a depreciation followed by an appreciation will leave the price level higher than it would otherwise have been. A recent paper (Kuran, 1983) provides new theoretical support for the notion that firms may react asymmetrically to pressures for price rises and falls, with similar incentives generating a larger rise than fall.

There have been several empirical attempts to detect such a ratchet effect. Goldstein (1980, pp. 13–17) provided a careful survey of this literature. He found conclusive evidence that import prices decline in appreciating currencies and no evidence of an asymmetry with the rise in depreciating currencies. He also concluded that the econometric evidence is not favorable to the hypothesis that increases in costs have a significantly different effect on prices than decreases. He therefore concluded that the hypothesis is without empirical support. This is perhaps convincing if one is assessing the effects of short-run *volatility* of the exchange rate, where induced price changes might not have time to affect wage claims. But the finding is certainly not decisive so far as *misalignments* are concerned, inasmuch as all it shows is that no ratchet effect exists on *prices* for a given path of wages. Yet surely at least 80 percent of the concern about "downward price inflexibility" has always been about downward *wage* inflexibility, and specifically that a depreciation may encounter real wage resistance. Goldstein himself adds in a footnote:

If wage-rate indexation formulas are asymmetrical or if real-wage resistance in general is asymmetrical, depreciations will raise labor costs by more than equivalent appreciations will lower them, thus imparting an upward bias to the inflation rate. In such circumstances, however, it is not clear why exchange rates rather than the wage-setting rules themselves should be regarded as inflationary, since any factor that moves the price level up and down will add to inflation in such an environment.

If one were assigning blame among various social institutions, one might well place more odium on the relevant wage-setting practices than on the exchange rate regime. But if one wants to know whether large and persistent exchange rate swings have unfortunate effects in the world in which we live, the stylized facts of downward wage inflexibility and real wage resistance imply that the answer is "yes."[17] Weak empirical support for this presumption was presented by Kenen and Pack (1980, p. 20, table 1).

PROTECTIONISM   It can be persuasively argued on both theoretical and empirical grounds that overvaluations tend to generate strong protectionist pressures. The theoretical argument observes that protection is demanded by industries that can plausibly blame a decline in demand on foreign competition. Demand does of course vary in response to the business cycle as well as foreign competition, and it is widely believed that recession is the principal source of protectionist pressures. But the 20 percent decline in demand in a typical industry as a result of a severe recession can easily be dwarfed by the effect of a 20 percent fall in the price of imports. Moreover, in the latter case the imports *are* the source of the domestic industry's troubles. Furthermore, the protectionist coalition is likely to be far broader when it is not just the industrial cripples that find themselves unable to match import competition.

It may be asked whether there is not likely to be an offsetting pressure in favor of trade liberalization that comes into play when a currency is undervalued. Such an effect is possible, although one may doubt whether it will be as strong as the protectionist pressures that arise in times of

---

17. Indeed, with real wage resistance, a period of overvaluation may build in real wage aspirations that are not consistent with a subsequent return to full equilibrium, but instead would generate inflationary pressure at full employment and the former equilibrium real exchange rate. Suppose, for example, that a 30 percent real appreciation raises real wages by 10 percent. It might be that a subsequent depreciation would be allowed to cut real wages by 5 percent before encountering wage resistance, but that would still make a return to full macroeconomic equilibrium unattainable. This suggests that the tight money/overvalued exchange rate strategy of inflation control adopted *inter alia* by Margaret Thatcher and Martinez de Hoz may actually make it more difficult to return to noninflationary full employment.

overvaluation. But, in addition, resources may be induced to enter export- and import-competing industries because of the artificially favorable competitive position generated by undervaluation. When the undervaluation subsequently disappears, those industries may then have to seek import restrictions or subsidies to avoid sharp cutbacks in their scale of operation. Thus over time a sequence of overvaluation and undervaluation is likely to ratchet up the level of protection.

On the empirical level, Bergsten (1982) observes that the three major postwar episodes of tension in US-Japanese trade relations in 1970–71, 1977–78, and since 1981 all originated in periods of an overvalued dollar (especially in terms of the yen). The first of these episodes produced widespread congressional support for the protectionist Mills bill and Burke-Hartke bill, despite the fact that unemployment was low when those efforts began. Protectionist pressures remain severe at the present time in the United States, reflecting the overvalued dollar, and despite the recovery.

Misalignments Matter

In contrast to exchange rate volatility, which is a troublesome nuisance rather than a major source of concern, exchange rate misalignments undermine economic performance in several central dimensions: they may generate austerity, adjustment costs, recession, deindustrialization, inflation, and protectionism. The strange fact is that misalignments have rarely even been considered by economists as a possible consequence of floating. There seem to be two reasons for this. One is that the professional view of floating was largely molded by the experience of the Canadian dollar in the 1950s, when no major misalignment emerged.[18] It was indeed often taken as axiomatic that floating would serve to *avoid* misalignments. The other is that major misalignments are typically most easily explained by some inept piece of macroeconomic policy making (e.g., the US creation of a structural budget deficit, precipitate Japanese abolition of capital export controls, UK monetary and fiscal tightening when oil price increases were causing an attempt to shift into sterling) rather than as the result of any intrinsic dynamics of floating exchange rates, such as "bandwagon effects" or responsiveness of

---

18. There was some concern in Canada at the appreciation of the Canadian dollar in the mid-1950s, but this was mild indeed compared to experience since 1973.

exchange rates to current accounts which in turn respond with a long lag to exchange rates.

But is it really true that floating would be vindicated by a finding that misalignments emerge only because countries adopt foolish policies? Not necessarily. If one starts with a presupposition that countries should choose their fiscal and monetary policies without regard to what is happening abroad, then one can hardly avoid endorsing floating rates, for this is indeed the only regime capable of reconciling uncoordinated policies. But the question is whether countries *ought* to select their policies in this way. Not only does the fact that we live in an interdependent world, where the policies adopted in one country have profound impacts on the course of events elsewhere, imply that countries have a responsibility to consider the interests of their partners, but the attempt to pursue policies that will not be acceptable to others is likely to lead to actions that are against the country's own long-run interests. It is a failing of the floating regime that the pressures to coordinate policies are so weak that countries have had the leeway to adopt policies so internationally inconsistent as to generate severe misalignments. Attempts to manage exchange rates would focus attention on causes of international inconsistency, like the structural fiscal deficit in the United States, and make it that much harder for such policy aberrations to be tolerated.

Since the major problem posed by floating rates is the emergence of misalignments, the major emphasis of policy should be on limiting the size of misalignments. This is not to say that reduced volatility would not also be desirable: in fact lower volatility and lesser misalignments are likely to prove complementary, since not only would smaller volatility reduce the noise in the exchange rate that helps generate and sustain misalignments, but greater confidence that future misalignments will be avoided would help pin down the rate in the short run. But the basic focus of exchange rate management should be on estimating an appropriate value for the exchange rate and seeking to limit deviations from that value beyond a reasonable range. It will be assumed in what follows that management is indeed directed to that end.

Causes of Misalignments

If management is to be directed to limiting misalignments, it is important to consider the possible causes of misalignments. Since a misalignment has been defined as a deviation of the market rate from fundamental equilibrium, it can arise for any of three reasons (or from some combination of the three):

• a deviation of the market rate from the market equilibrium, which would occur as a result of what might be termed *misguided intervention*

• a deviation of market equilibrium from current equilibrium, which occurs as a result of what is customarily termed *market inefficiency*

• a deviation of current equilibrium from fundamental equilibrium, as a result of the stance of *macroeconomic policy*.

MISGUIDED INTERVENTION   Clearly one cannot rule out the possibility that intervention (or other policies directed at influencing the exchange rate) might *create* rather than limit a misalignment. Indeed, charges have sometimes been made that central banks systematically lose money in intervening and, by implication, that these policies tend·to destabilize exchange rates (e.g., Taylor, 1982).

The Jurgensen Report (1983) considered these criticisms, but rejected them for two reasons. First, it challenged the conclusion that intervention has typically lost money (para. 76). It pointed out that, in calculating the profitability of intervention, Taylor had valued the dollars acquired in intervention at their value at the end of the period he studied, at which time the dollar happened to be undervalued. If one extrapolates Taylor's calculations forward into the period of a strong dollar, one gets contrary results. But that result too is misleading: a correct assessment requires that one calculate the profitability of intervention over a period when intervention has balanced out, so that terminal stocks are the same as initial stocks, thus sidestepping the problem of valuing the terminal (and initial) stocks of foreign exchange. The Jurgensen Report stated that such studies have been made in official circles and affirmed that most such calculations have shown intervention to have been profitable. A published example of these studies is Mayer and Taguchi (1983).

The second reason the Jurgensen Report rejected the charge that official intervention has been a costly failure is that it accepted the contention of Mayer and Taguchi that intervention could be unprofitable but nonetheless stabilizing. A simple way of seeing the basic point is to consider the case where the authorities succeed in stabilizing the rate perfectly, in which case they would make zero profits. But if they marginally "overstabilized" they would make a loss, no matter how great the instability that would have occurred in the absence of intervention.

Despite that qualification, the evidence that intervention has in general been profitable does suggest that it has not usually been "misguided," in the sense of amplifying misalignments. Nevertheless, there have been instances of the latter. One way in which such instances can arise is through countries' pursuing intervention policies of the "leaning-against-the-wind" variety when a misalignment is being *corrected* (rather than created), as happened *inter alia* with Japan in 1976. This demonstrates the inappropriateness of leaning against the wind as a strategic guide to intervention policy, given that the major object of policy should be to limit misalignments. For that purpose the authorities cannot escape taking a view of the appropriate rate (or range of rates).

Most instances of misguided intervention could probably have been avoided had the authorities given explicit consideration to the choice of an appropriate real exchange rate target. But there is at least one case where the authorities had sought to estimate such a target and nevertheless intervened in a way that was obviously (in retrospect) misguided: namely, the British attempt to cap the rise in sterling in 1977. Appendix figure A11 indicates that the rate the authorities attempted to defend in mid-1977 was below the FEER. This suggests two morals. The first is the danger of allowing recent experience— in that case, the experience of the speculative crisis of 1976—an excessive weight in influencing judgments of the long-run concept of fundamental equilibrium. The second is the desirability of allowing a wide range around the preferred FEER to accommodate reasonable doubts about its true value. Had those precepts been respected, Britain would have avoided the misfortune of buying up large quantities of dollars at a very high (sterling) price, in the process subjecting itself to unwanted monetary pressures as well as losing money on the operation.

MARKET INEFFICIENCY   Popular and political discussion of exchange rates frequently blames "speculators" for "selling currencies short," creating "bandwagon effects," and causing "overshooting."[19] Professional econo-

---

19. "Overshooting" has often been used as synonymous with what is here described as a "misalignment." Some of us regret this deviation from Dornbusch's (1976) original usage, where the term described a situation where the market and current equilibrium (which were identical in his model, due to the assumption of perfect foresight) temporarily moved more than the fundamental (nominal) equilibrium (following a shock that altered the latter) for the quite specific purpose of maintaining interest parity in the presence of sticky prices.

mists have typically gone to the other extreme, arguing that speculators play a socially beneficial role in ensuring that the latest information is incorporated in exchange rates, that foreign exchange markets are efficient, that expectations are rational,[20] and that, if bandwagon effects really existed, they would present unexploited profit opportunities to speculators.

There have been a series of attempts to test the hypothesis that the foreign exchange market is efficient since the advent of floating a decade ago. The most recent and most authoritative of these were commissioned by the Working Group on Exchange Market Intervention. The relevant paragraphs of the resulting report (Jurgensen Report, 1983, paras. 61–66) are worth quoting in full:

The value of intervention in stabilising exchange rates depends to a critical extent on the working of the exchange market and its role in the process of exchange rate determination. For this reason, the Working Group examined in detail the extent to which exchange markets are "efficient" in the sense that they take account of all information which is relevant for the determination of exchange rates. If exchange markets rapidly and fully assimilated such information and translated it into appropriate spot and forward rate levels, there would be one less reason for monetary authorities to intervene directly in the markets. Efficient exchange markets would not, for example, allow repetitive bandwagon-type exchange rate movements to emerge.

Empirical tests of exchange-market efficiency are based on the propositions that: (a) transaction costs are minimal; (b) all relevant information is utilised by exchange market participants; and (c) assets denominated in different currencies are perfectly substitutable in private portfolios. If all three propositions are satisfied, then the forward exchange rate should constitute the best available predictor of the future spot rate. On these assumptions, the use of any other variables such as inflation and interest rate differentials should not produce better forecasting results than the forward rate nor should the consistent application of simple exchange trading rules using these variables yield positive returns. Both suppositions were tested empirically.

The tests provided clear evidence that consideration of readily accessible information on inflation and interest rate differentials yielded a better prediction of the future spot rate than that implied by the forward rate. Moreover, the repeated application of

---

20. Expectations are said to be "rational" when those involved have a correct perception of how the world works ("know the structure of the model") and make the best possible use of all available information to forecast the future. The attraction of the concept is that, if everyone has such expectations and acts on them, the expectations will prove self-fulfilling. Rational expectations are the stochastic analogue of perfect foresight. See Begg (1982) for an excellent introduction and survey of the now-abundant literature.

certain foreign exchange trading rules indicated a high probability of making some profit. However, some members thought that the results for some currencies may have been affected by the existence of capital controls, although the results were similar for the six bilateral US dollar rates tested. Other time series studies performed by the Group confirmed the existence of better predictors of the future spot rate than the forward rate.

This evidence can have three different explanations, which are not necessarily mutually exclusive. As transaction costs are usually neither very large nor particularly variable, it is generally thought that they do not explain the observed results. Consequently, the test suggests that markets are inefficient and/or that investors require time-varying risk premia because assets in different currencies are not perfect substitutes for one another. Views differed among the members of the Working Group as to how to interpret this outcome. Those members who were inclined to attribute the existence of systematic and exploitable prediction errors primarily to variable exchange risk premia considered it highly implausible that exchange market participants should systematically ignore low-cost information that is relevant to the determination of the exchange rate. Other members tended to interpret the result of the empirical tests as evidence of exchange market inefficiency. Their view was based on the general failure of empirical studies conducted to date to produce evidence that would explain potential risk premia entirely in terms of their theoretical determinants. Moreover, relevant information might be ignored by market participants as a result of the high cost of properly processing it. Thus, expectations might be rational in the everyday sense of the word although not conforming to the technical concept of efficiency.

Doubts about the efficiency of exchange markets have also been expressed in most case studies of exchange rate developments—at least to the extent that bandwagon effects can be regarded as a sign of exchange market inefficiency. All countries had identified bandwagon movements at particular times, and some countries intervened to forestall the emergence of bandwagon effects. For example, Canada had seen the risk in July and August 1981 that the decline in the Canadian dollar might feed on itself, and the UK authorities had been concerned to prevent any fall in the pound sterling from becoming self-sustaining in June to October 1981. Japan stated that there had been several periods in which bandwagon effects had been very much in evidence. In particular, between January and October 1978 the yen was said to have risen continuously on several occasions without any significant new information having been supplied to the market, and the upward movement in the exchange rate on one day appeared to have been the determinant of the yen's appreciation on the following day. Italy interpreted erratic exchange rate movements at the end of February 1976 as raising a suspicion that bandwagon effects were at work.

The Working Group noted that the test results indicated that intervention may have had a significant impact on exchange rates—irrespective of whether markets are inefficient or whether variable exchange risk premia exist. If markets are inefficient in the sense that they fail to assign appropriate weight to information on macroeconomic variables in determining exchange rates, action to influence the exchange rate including intervention could be an effective component of macroeconomic policies. In this case intervention would have an impact through its influence on expectations—for example, its demonstration effect—about future underlying economic conditions or policies. Alternatively, if exchange markets are efficient and unexploited profits are indicative of time-varying risk premia, intervention could still be an effective policy tool. This would be so because official operations in the exchange market, by changing the currency composition of private portfolios, would alter risk exposures in the various currencies and thus have a lasting effect on exchange rates.

In other words, there is serious reason to doubt whether exchange markets are efficient. One cannot legitimately take it for granted that the market rate will always approximate current equilibrium.[21] Some intriguing explanations as to why exchange markets may at times generate exchange rates bearing no systematic relationship to current equilibrium are starting to emerge. Rudiger Dornbusch (1983, pp. 18–20) has perhaps the most comprehensive succinct discussion of such explanations to date:

The first is familiar from the recent literature on financial markets and concerns the possibility that exchange rates, in part, are determined by irrelevant information. Market participants may have the wrong model of fundamentals, and their expectations, based on the wrong model, will affect the actual exchange rate. If there is sufficiently high serial correlation in the irrelevant variables, it may be impossible to discern the systematic forecast errors using conventional efficiency tests. But the exchange rate will be significantly more volatile than is warranted by the true model.

This point is important because market participants may be impressed by a plausible fundamental variable, attribute explanatory power to it, and, consequently, make their expectations actually come true. Then, when some other variable moves, attention may shift to a different "main factor," which, in turn, comes to dominate the exchange rate for a while.

---

21. Note that "time-varying risk premia"—or low asset substitutability, in language that is still more familiar to some—influences the deviation of current equilibrium from fundamental equilibrium rather than that of market equilibrium from current equilibrium. That is, with imperfect asset substitutability a change in interest rates will lead to a different change in current equilibrium to that which would occur with perfect asset substitutability. Comment on the potential role of low asset substitutability in contributing to deviation of the market rate from fundamental equilibrium is therefore reserved until the next subsection.

Exchange rates carried by irrelevant beliefs are troublesome, not only because of the excess variance but also because shifting from one irrelevant factor to another will precipitate major exchange rate collapses. The possibility that exchange rates are sometimes far out of line with the fundamentals cannot be discounted. It is important to recognize this, because in the past economists may have given excessive weight to the notion that the market knows "the model" and, at the same time, is rational. It is quite conceivable that a number of fashionable factors, such as fiscal discipline, basic monetary control, long-run strength in manufacturing, *Angebotsfreundliche Gesellschaftspolitik* (supply side policy) play a role, one at a time.

The second source of disequilibrium exchange rates is expectations about the possibility of regime changes and has been called the "peso problem." In this perspective exchange rates are influenced not only by current fundamentals but also by agents' expectations that there are given probabilities that fundamentals may change in specific directions. If market participants have sufficiently strong beliefs that a given course of policy will not be followed, they may, in fact, make it impossible for the authorities to follow that course. Under flexible exchange rates, this problem may become acute because the exchange rate is so flexible a price and so much governed by expectations. It may well be argued, as was done in the discussion of the French stabilization experience under Poincaré, that speculators are the true judges of fundamentals and that a collapse of the exchange rate brought about by adverse capital flows is irrevocable evidence of a program of stabilization that was out of touch with fundamentals. But such an argument must be viewed as simplistic by anyone who recognizes that stabilization policy has a wide range of indeterminacy.

The third source of disequilibrium exchange rates can be explained using the analogy of bubbles. A bubble exists when holders of an asset realize that the asset is overpriced but are nevertheless willing to hold it, since they believe there is only a limited risk of a price collapse during a given holding period; therefore, asset holders expect to be able to sell eventually at a price that will provide them with sufficient capital gains to compensate them for running the risk of a collapse. An analogous situation occurs when a currency has appreciated more than can be considered justified by fundamentals and overvaluation is widely thought to prevail, but appreciation is expected to continue until some disturbance causes the crash. There are no models of such a crash as yet, but it should be clear that an essential ingredient is the arrival of new information that diverts a sufficient number of speculators from keeping the bubble growing.

There is also quite a widespread feeling among those in contact with the foreign exchange markets that the behavior of the current account plays a larger role in determining exchange rates than is allowed by the currently dominant strand of economic theorizing. It is maintained that, rather than peering into the distant future to make well-informed forecasts of how the current account will respond to the exchange rate, the market takes its cue from the actual contemporaneous behavior of the current account, even when this is distorted by the J-curve or other temporary phenomena. It is easy to see that such behavior can generate self-perpetuating cycles in the exchange rate. A depreciated rate eventually creates a surplus, which causes the rate to appreciate. Since this initially enlarges the surplus (because of the J-curve), the rate "overshoots" (in a general sense of the term, rather than in Dornbusch's technical sense), which ultimately causes a deficit, which leads to an excessive depreciation, and so on.

An imaginative paper by Schulmeister (1983) tries to integrate this type of idea with those of interest arbitrage and "bandwagon effects." For a time the market may be willing to finance a current account deficit (for example) because of a higher interest rate offered by the deficit country, but the longer this persists, the more uneasy will the market become. Eventually the exchange rate starts to slip, and as it does so more and more speculators jump on the bandwagon. The rate stabilizes again only when it has so overshot the equilibrium level as to raise worries that it may start to rebound.

Such theories as these have not yet been fully articulated and appraised, nor have they been absorbed into the mainstream of economic thought—let alone subjected to rigorous empirical testing. But Nurkse's (1944) warning about the characteristics of speculative conduct in foreign exchange markets now looks a lot less far-fetched than it was generally rated a decade ago. As Keynes (1936, p. 156) argued with his analogy to a beauty contest in which the winner is whoever comes closest to guessing the popular order, conduct that is quite rational for individual participants may in a speculative market add up to social behavior that appears wildly irrational. All of this suggests that exchange markets may experience severe misalignments as a result of market equilibrium deviating from current equilibrium.

MACROECONOMIC POLICY   But there is yet another way in which misalignments can arise: from macroeconomic policy's pushing current equilibrium away from fundamental equilibrium. For example, a country may embark on a program of determined monetary restraint as a means of ridding itself of inflation. Unless accompanied by complementary fiscal and incomes policies, such a program will entail a rise in real interest rates and hence a real appreciation (as has been seen in recent years in both Britain and the United States). Conversely, an attempt to stimulate demand by unbalanced monetary expansion will lead to a real depreciation.

How great the misalignment caused by such a policy proves to be depends on the degree of asset substitutability. In the case of perfect substitutability beloved by economic theorists, an expectation that real interest rates were going to remain 4 percent above those abroad during a three-year period of disinflation would cause the current equilibrium exchange rate to appreciate by 12 percent.

The movements of real effective exchange rates shown in the appendix figures suggest that changes have at times of severe disinflation been much larger than this. One interesting question is whether this could be explained by imperfect substitutability. This possibility seems to have been largely disregarded by many economists, apparently on the rather casual ground that the speculative capital flows prior to an expected change in a pegged exchange rate can be enormous. What this overlooks is that the *incentive* to shift funds out of a currency about to be devalued is astronomical too. Someone who shifted funds from the French franc to the DM for the weekend of their recent 8 percent realignment earned 3½ percent in two days, an annualized yield of 45,643 percent! It is no wonder that a lot of money moves when faced with such an incentive,[22] but this tells us nothing useful about asset substitutability.

It has to be said that it is not clear that imperfect asset substitutability is capable of explaining why exchange rates change so much in response to interest differentials. The usual view would be that a 1 percent rise in the dollar interest differential would have *less* effect if assets are worse substitutes, since it would motivate a smaller attempt to shift into dollars. Paul S. Armington (1981) has argued, however, that investors value the interest component of the yield of an asset more highly than the capital gain component because of the high degree of uncertainty that attaches to the latter. Although this argument seems intuitively plausible, it has not yet been given a respectable theoretical base. Until this matter is clarified, it would be wrong to attach excessive weight to the apparent fact that exchange rates overreact to changes in interest differentials. But it would also be wrong to ignore the possibility that a reform of the exchange rate mechanism that served to reduce the uncertainty attaching to longer run exchange rate

---

22. It is also reported that short-term interest rates rose so high in France that someone who got the timing wrong and borrowed francs to shift funds to the DM two weeks before the realignment occurred would have lost money on the operation. This does not alter the basic point that the incentives involved are an order of magnitude larger than those encountered in routine financial management (nor does it reassure one that such circumstances can be anything but disruptive).

movements could drastically cut the misalignments that result from a given interest rate differential.

Costs of Limiting Misalignments

If misalignments are caused primarily by misguided intervention, their elimination would be costless: all that would be necessary would be for the authorities to abstain from such intervention. The evidence does not, however, suggest that such a free ride is available. To the extent that misalignments are caused by market inefficiency or macroeconomic policy, any limitation of misalignments might require a deliberate willingness to sacrifice other policy objectives. The sacrifice actually involved might prove to be minimal where misalignments arise because of inefficiency, or if exaggerated misalignments result from modest interest differentials because of low asset substitutability. The "sacrifice" may also turn out to be a blessing in disguise to the extent that the management of exchange rates forces an international coordination of economic policy that is needed for everyone's long-run good but would not otherwise occur. But even in that case policymakers will want to know what freedom they would need to give up in order to manage the exchange rate to limit misalignments.

The case for a managed exchange rate is distinct from the case for either a fixed or a floating exchange rate, either of which can generate misalignments. Unlike a fixed exchange rate, a managed rate can be so managed as to neutralize inflation differentials (thus preventing misalignments emerging from differential inflation) or to change the real exchange rate, when that would be helpful either to promote adjustment to a long-lasting change in real circumstances or to react to an abnormal temporary (e.g., cyclical) situation. Unlike a freely floating exchange rate, a managed rate allows the possibility of absorbing variations in the desire to hold different currencies in changes in the supplies of the various currencies, rather than in their prices (exchange rates). Management can therefore prevent such shifts in portfolio preferences from generating misalignments.

The costs of managing exchange rates to limit misalignments depend upon both the technique adopted for that purpose and the regime with which managed rates are compared. It is argued in the next section that, while other techniques, like sterilized intervention, may be able to give limited assistance, a serious commitment to exchange rate management leaves no realistic alternative to a willingness to direct monetary policy at least in part toward an exchange rate target. The nature of the sacrifices involved in adopting such a strategy may best be understood by comparison with the two textbook regimes of fixed and freely floating exchange rates.

MANAGED VERSUS FIXED RATES   Fixed exchange rates are more effective than managed rates in reducing short-run volatility and in producing certainty in long-run *nominal* comparisons. Managed rates produce more certainty in *real* comparisons. If the earlier argument regarding the relative significance of misalignments and volatility is accepted, this difference indicates an advantage for managed rates.

About the only traditional argument in favor of fixed rates that continues to apply against managed rates is that a fixed rate serves to anchor the national price level. If a small country pegs its exchange rate to the currency of a large trading partner and then pursues those policies—notably monetary policy—needed to maintain the peg constant, there is no doubt that the inflation rate of the small country will tend to follow that of its large partner, at least in the long run. For suppose that inflation were too high: then arbitrage pressures from abroad would start to discipline domestic prices directly, the country would lose reserves and the money supply would fall, and unemployment would rise (on account of both the unfavorable trade balance resulting from uncompetitive exports and the cut in spending resulting from monetary stringency) and discipline wage increases. Provided that the country stuck to its fixed exchange rate—which may mean allowing the money supply to fall, and create a recession—inflation would eventually be brought back into line.

A country that manages its exchange rate with a view to preserving price competitiveness cuts itself off from this discipline. If its inflation starts off being higher than abroad, it depreciates its currency to neutralize that excess inflation and creates enough additional money to ensure that the depreciation actually occurs. Thus all the stabilizing forces that drag inflation back down under a fixed exchange rate are ruptured. Worse still, if a country did not start off with excess inflation but decided to hold its exchange rate at a more undervalued level than was consistent with equilibrium of the real economy, a policy of rigidly managing the exchange rate to preserve competitiveness would lead to an explosive inflation.

Any country that plans to manage its real exchange rate therefore needs to be certain that it has an adequate alternative to an exchange rate peg as a means of controlling inflation. That alternative must include a willingness to take domestic measures—including a willingness to adopt restrictive fiscal measures to a point where, if all else fails, unemployment rises—in response to a rise in inflation. It must also include a willingness to adjust the target for the real exchange rate if there is evidence that the target has been set at a level inconsistent with equilibrium of the real economy.

The strategy of using domestic demand-management policy rather than a pegged exchange rate to control inflation will seem more natural to large and relatively closed economies than to the small open economy. But even in the latter case there is much to be said for it. The "global monetarist" claim that inflation could be controlled on the cheap by pegging the exchange rate and relying on arbitrage—the "Law of One Price"—has been decisively discredited by the experiences of Argentina and Chile (Ardito-Barletta, 1983). It is now abundantly clear (as it always should have been) that controlling inflation by pegging the exchange rate involves the same painful process of allowing unemployment to rise as is involved in the domestic route to inflation control. The difference is that inflation control through foreign competition concentrates the recession on the internationally competitive sector, which undermines medium-term prospects and offends conventional canons of equality of sacrifice. A country that has enough discipline to stick to an exchange rate peg when inflationary pressures develop can just as well take the domestic measures needed to restore price stability.

MANAGED VERSUS FREE-FLOATING RATES   The fact remains that a country abandoning the external inflation anchor does need a domestic replacement. If fiscal and incomes policies are ruled out for ideological reasons as being too "Keynesian," the only alternative is a monetary growth rule. That is, of course, the solution favored by many advocates of free floating. Many of the arguments traditionally deployed in favor of floating rather than fixed rates are irrelevant in the present context—in particular, managed rates are just as capable of neutralizing differential inflation and of contributing to the adjustment process as are floating rates. But the assignment of monetary policy to domestic or exchange rate objectives remains at the heart of the issue.

Harry G. Johnson (1969) was one of those who used to claim that the central advantage of floating was the liberation of monetary policy to pursue "domestic objectives." Keynesian floaters regard the pursuit of domestic objectives as the choice of an interest rate appropriate to securing the right level and composition (between consumption and investment) of demand.[23]

---

23. Keynes himself certainly believed this freedom to use interest rates for domestic demand management to be of crucial importance: see Keynes (1936, p. 349).

Monetarist floaters interpret pursuing domestic objectives as securing a fixed rate of growth of the money supply. Both regard the need to defend an exchange rate as diverting monetary policy from its primary task.

Obviously one can accept the contention that monetary policy has important domestic objectives without abandoning the conviction that it should also be influenced by considerations of external competitiveness. The position advocated in this study is not that monetary policy should be directed solely to managing the exchange rate, but rather that it should seek to strike a balance between the need to manage the domestic economy and the need to limit misalignments.

Opposition to this view seems to come from two distinct, both extreme, parts of the monetarist spectrum. On the one side are those global monetarists with a misplaced confidence that, because of the "Law of One Price," everything that can be accomplished by monetary policy is achieved by pegging the exchange rate. On the other hand are those free floaters who argue that allowing considerations of external competitiveness to influence monetary policy has to be justified by special claims to superior knowledge on the part of the authorities. Thus Steven W. Kohlhagen (1982, p. 24) recently wrote:

For official intervention to make sense, central banks must either have more infomation than the market (and be willing to act correctly on it in a way that affects market prices) or have a more socially optimal taste for risk than the market collectively. How many central banks have a good sense of society's optimal risk preference or the market's actual taste for risk and know how to intervene to correct for any deviation between the two at a given time? If central banks have information that the market does not have, how do or should they use it? Why not release it? Only if that is impossible does it make sense perhaps to intervene and push the rate in the inevitable direction. But if the information never becomes public, or the central bank was wrong about its effect, or new information or new economic conditions negate or swamp the old information, such intervention can be destabilizing rather than stabilizing.

Why do central bankers feel that they know whether or not the market rate is correct? In point of fact, there is no right rate at any specific time. The correct exchange rate is the one that will bring about external equilibrium in the desired time period, given current information and risk aversion. The market's notion of the "desired time period" may not be the social optimum, but is the central bank's? Who should determine it? Should the soon-to-be-evident US deficit be corrected in two quarters, one year, or two years? As there is no "right rate," what target should a central bank adopt for intervention?

It is certainly possible to visualize circumstances where Kohlhagen would be correct. In a country that conducted its monetary policy according to a rigid monetarist rule of predetermining a constant growth rate of the money supply, the central bank could hope to improve on the judgment of the market only if it has access to superior knowledge or if the private market suffers from some pathological state such as socially excessive risk aversion or time discounting, or a propensity to engage in speculative runs. And if one believes that the best monetary policy is a fixed rate of monetary growth irrespective of circumstances, for example because one believes that only unanticipated monetary policy can influence output and that it does that by cheating the public, then one can logically advocate free floating on the grounds that Kohlhagen does.

But suppose instead that one believes that good monetary management can help to stabilize output by offsetting shocks emanating from the private sector. Then the authorities have to decide what set of policies will best further that objective. The market will of course set the exchange rate in the light of the policies chosen, and its expectations of future policies. Suppose that the central bank and the market have identical information and that both know the correct model, in the now-traditional rational expectations scenario (see footnote 20). Then if the authorities decide to set monetary policy solely with a view to best achieving the internal balance objective, that is what they will tend to achieve, since by hypothesis they will build in the correct private sector reactions to their policy. But given that there is in general a conflict between internal needs and external competitiveness, that is not the optimum policy, which involves striking a balance between both. Specifically, it involves taking account of where the exchange rate should be in order to generate an appropriate long-term level of competitiveness. The key point is that the authorities, unlike the private market, have macroeconomic objectives, and need to concern themselves with *all* the implications of the policies they adopt. The exchange rate is too important to be treated as the residual.

This is a position that seems quite congenial to a number of economists who would consider themselves monetarists (as well as to many who would not identify with that label). For example, the influential British financial journalist Samuel Brittan has repeatedly urged that pursuit of a target rate of monetary growth should be overridden where necessary to keep the exchange rate within reasonable bounds. The distinctly monetarist Swiss National Bank, and to a lesser extent the Bundesbank, actually applied such an override when the Swiss franc and DM appreciated to a damaging degree in late 1978. One of the leading monetarists at Chicago, Michael Mussa (1981,

p. 16), has argued that the authorities can be presumed to have an informational advantage in that "the central bank possesses a certainty of knowledge about its future monetary policy and its relationship to the behavior of exchange rates that is not available to private market participants." Alexandre Lamfalussy (1981) has similarly argued that "intervention means that the authorities are putting their money where their mouth is."

Kohlhagen is correct in arguing that the case for the authorities seeking to manage the exchange rate rests on their being able to "know whether or not the market rate is correct." But he is quite wrong in suggesting that this demands superior knowledge on their part, for what they need to ask themselves is not whether the rate approximates *current* equilibrium but how it stands in relation to *fundamental* equilibrium. The market simply does not ask itself what rate can be expected to clear the flow market for foreign exchange over any specific time period, optimal or otherwise, as Kohlhagen seems to imagine. Rather, the market sets a rate which equates the desire to hold different currencies with the current supplies, where those desires are influenced *inter alia* by market expectations of what is going to happen in future, including expectations of how attractive policy is going to make it to hold different currencies at various dates in the future. If one wishes the foreign exchange market to bring about external equilibrium over some even remotely optimal time period, one has no alternative but to figure out what that period is and what set of macroeconomic policies will induce the market to choose a rate consistent with achieving equilibrium over that period. In other words, one needs to estimate the FEER and manage the rate to approximate it!

There is something of a mystery as to how the market is supposed to be capable of pinning down the exchange rate to a value consistent with fundamental equilibrium in the long run, as supposed in much of the technical economic literature, if governments are unable to assess the approximate level of fundamental equilibrium. Note that there is a basic difference between a fish market and the foreign exchange market as regards the information sets available to the market on the one hand and the authorities on the other. In a fish market, market participants collectively know all there is to know about demand and supply; the government does not, and hence one can safely predict that a government attempt to fix prices will end in a mess. In the foreign exchange market, both market participants and governments have to resort to essentially similar speculation about the level of fundamental equilibrium. One reason for wanting governments to focus on the issue is that in doing so they would not be distracted by all the other considerations that inevitably concern market participants, like forecasting future government policy or the possibility of riding a speculative bandwagon.

Another reason for wanting governments to focus on the question of identifying FEERs and limiting deviations from them is the belief that this would lead to a better balance in policy formation. It is true that, as Gottfried Haberler (1983) has recently argued, the emergence of an exchange rate misalignment *may* stimulate a government to take needed policy actions— e.g., the role of the weak dollar in motivating a shift to anti-inflationary policies in the United States in 1978–79. But it would surely be better if governments were forced to act by the *need to prevent misalignments from emerging* rather than to try to correct the damage done once a misalignment has emerged. Not only would this lead to a prompter acceptance of needed policy changes, but it should contribute to a better policy mix. The present excessive level of real interest rates could hardly have arisen had governments not been able to treat the exchange rate as a residual and thus relax their concern to maintain a proper balance between fiscal and monetary policy.

Benefits and Costs of Exchange Rate Management

It has been argued in this section that the major costs of floating exchange rates stem from the misalignments that they have allowed to emerge, rather than from the annoyance of high volatility. Those costs were identified as an alternation of splurge and austerity, adjustment costs, unemployment in the tradable goods industries, deindustrialization, a ratchet effect on inflation, and protectionist pressures. Although there has been little systematic work directed to measuring those costs, the presumption is that they are large, and provide a significant part of the explanation for the weak economic performance of the world in the decade since floating was adopted.

The costs of attempting to curb the costs of free floating depend on why misalignments arise. There is no practical way of decomposing the responsibility for misalignments among the three possible causes identified, namely, misguided intervention, market inefficiency, and macroeconomic policy, although there seems reason to believe that both of the last two factors have been important. To the extent that market inefficiency is the source of the problem, exchange rate management need not involve any systematic sacrifice of internal policy objectives, although it will require a willingness to direct policy toward exchange rate management rather than to let the exchange rate be the residual. But where macroeconomic policy is responsible, governments may face a real choice between the monetary policy that is appropriate for internal versus external objectives. If they decide to give some weight to external objectives, they need to wield a sufficiently comprehensive set of policy instruments to ensure that the main internal objectives can still be attained, most specifically to ensure the control of inflation. There is, however, a converse side to this argument: namely, that the attempt to achieve domestic and external objectives simultaneously will create pressures for a balanced policy mix, which is likely to be beneficial both to a country's partners and, in the long run, to itself.

4   Techniques of Exchange Rate Management

The preceding section identified two crucial conditions that must be satisfied if a country is to manage its exchange rate with a view to limiting misalignments. First, it must make sure that it has an adequate "anchor" to prevent inflation from taking off. Abandonment of both the traditional anchors, a fixed nominal exchange rate peg and a fixed monetary growth rule, can only be undertaken safely provided there is a firm commitment to a balanced use of domestic demand policy to control inflation.

For example, so long as the United States is unwilling to use fiscal policy to ensure that inflation does not revive, that burden will have to be carried by monetary policy, which will curtail the extent to which monetary policy can be directed toward the exchange rate. The case for nevertheless seeking a move toward greater exchange rate management in the United States at the present time rests on the twin hopes that this would increase the pressure for a more responsible fiscal policy and that the mere delineation of objectives might make some contribution toward modifying the overvaluation of the dollar.

The second precondition for a policy of exchange rate management to make sense is that the authorities possess a reasonable ability to identify the fundamental equilibrium exchange rate. This is an exercise that used to be undertaken routinely in the days of the Bretton Woods system, whenever a par value change was considered. It is an exercise that many countries continue to perform regularly, and in which the IMF takes a keen interest and claims considerable expertise when it comes to dealing with small deficit countries with pegged exchange rates. It is an exercise that on one occasion, prior to the Smithsonian Agreement of December 1971, formed the basis of a major and ultimately successful diplomatic negotiation.[24] And it is an exercise that could be performed again on a multilateral basis if the will were there; the necessary techniques were used to estimate FEERs in section 2. It may not prove possible to diagnose FEERs with any great degree of accuracy, but approximate figures would suffice to support a great improvement in performance.

Not only must the authorities possess the *ability* to diagnose FEERs to a useful degree of approximation, but they must be prepared to exercise that ability and abandon the silly pretense that the exchange rate is none of their business. Any strategy intended to limit misalignments requires the authorities to develop a view of where the exchange rate would need to be to achieve a level of competitiveness that would be sustainable and appropriate in the long run. This view may be expressed as a real rate—in which case it will have to be translated into the nominal rate implied by prevailing price levels before the policy implications are apparent. Or it may be expressed as a nominal rate—in which case it will have to be adjusted regularly in response to differential inflation. It may be published, in the form of a central target or of a band or range. Or it may be treated as confidential. But in some form or other the authorities must have, and recognize at least to themselves that they have, what one may naturally term a "target" for the level of the exchange rate. That is the basic minimum condition for any attempt to manage the exchange rate to limit misalignments. (A policy of "leaning against the wind" designed simply to slow down any exchange rate change does not require the authorities to develop any view as to the correct level, but neither can it be expected to limit misalignments in any systematic way.)

Having persuaded themselves that the exchange rate is a topic on which they owe it to the public to take a view, the authorities would have to make a series of further decisions:

---

24. At least, the negotiation was successful in achieving agreement, though that agreement lasted little over a year. The FEERs calculated in section 2, together with the figures in table 10, suggest that there was good reason for the Smithsonian Agreement to break down: the dollar and the yen remained misaligned by over 10 percent and the DM by almost 10 percent.

- whether to commit themselves to a peg with formal margins, or to float with a "target zone" with "soft margins"

- how wide any band or target zone should be

- how the target rate should be changed

- whether to publish their target rate

- what policy instruments should be used to limit deviations of the exchange rate from its target.

Pegging versus Floating

An exchange rate is said to be "pegged" if the authorities accept an obligation to prevent the market rate from deviating by more than a specified amount (called the "margin") from the peg. Twice the margins gives the band, the maximum range within which the exchange rate is allowed to move without a change in the peg (or central rate).

An exchange rate is said to "float" if the authorities do not accept an obligation to limit the range of the market rate. It floats "freely" or "cleanly" if the authorities do not take any actions designed to influence the behavior of the exchange rate. It is said to be "managed" if the authorities attempt to influence the behavior of the rate without committing themselves to hold it within a specified range.

"Target zones" seem to mean different things to different people. To some they mean a wide band. To others they mean an unpublished band. To others the word "zone" is used with the deliberate purpose of providing a *contrast* to the word "band," to indicate a range beyond which the authorities are unhappy to see the rate move, despite *not* being prepared to precommit themselves to prevent such movements. Since the first two concepts have straightforward alternative titles while the third is an important concept that lacks an alternative simple description, the term will be used in that latter sense here. It is important to understand that, in this sense, a system of target zones is a *form of floating*, rather than a form of pegging. Target zones have "soft margins" which the authorities are *not* committed to defending.

If one is thinking of providing a framework for a worldwide return to a structured exchange rate system, it seems clear that the greatest degree of commitment that it would be realistic to contemplate—at least in the first instance—is a system of target zones with soft margins. The United States, in particular, could not be expected to make a greater commitment of monetary policy to external objectives—and would be right in refusing any greater commitment, at least until fiscal policy is brought under control. This is not to exclude closer arrangements among some groups of countries, e.g., the EMS, nor the possibility of further moves at a later date.

Band or Zone Width

The considerations that are relevant in choosing the width of a formal band are rather different from those relevant to choosing the width of a target zone. A country that commits itself to defending specified margins needs to make sure that those margins are wide enough to allow it to adjust its central rate without provoking an exchange crisis, and wide enough to allow it to absorb an appropriate part of the temporary shocks it encounters in movements of the exchange rate.

The first point may be graphically illustrated by the differing experiences of France and Denmark in the last (March 1983) EMS realignment. France devalued by 8 percent relative to the deutschemark, the dominant currency in the EMS. As shown in figure 1, this meant that any speculator who bought DM from the Banque de France before the realignment, when the franc was at its weak margin at point C, and sold them afterwards when the franc was at its new strong margin at D, made a profit of 3½ percent. In contrast the Danish krone was devalued only by 3 percent. Hence the speculator who sold Danish kroner at point C (in the bottom part of the diagram) had to buy them back at point D and *lost* 1½ percent on the

FIGURE 1   **The EMS realignment of March 1983**

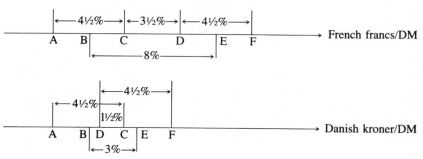

transaction. The moral is that, as long as the band width is greater than the change in the central rate, it is possible to adjust central rates without generating speculative crises. Since there is no minimum necessary size of changes in central rates, however, this does not really pose much of a constraint on the choice of band width, except in countries that have hang-ups about the frequency of changes in central rates.

A more important constraint arises from the desirability of being able to absorb certain shocks in the exchange rate without having to adjust the central rate. Suppose, for example, that there is a cyclical rise in the foreign interest rate which the domestic country does not wish to follow since it does not consider itself subject to inflationary pressure. Then it would wish to allow its currency to depreciate, to the point where the market considered the prospect of a subsequent appreciation sufficient compensation for continuing to hold the same stock of low-interest domestic assets. It is preferable to accommodate such temporary shocks by movements within the margins rather than by changes in central rates for several reasons: so as not to give misleading signals for resource allocation, so as not to lessen confidence in the probability of a subsequent rebound of the rate, and so as to allow the initial adjustment to a shock to be made instantaneously. How wide the margins needed for this purpose depends on how large the interest rate differentials likely to be needed to provide autonomy of domestic action. With perfect asset substitutability, an ability to hold a 3 percent interest differential for two years would require margins of 6 percent.

Although less critical in determining the width of a target zone, inasmuch as the rate can be allowed to float outside the soft margins when that appears expedient, both these considerations remain relevant. But the most important criterion relates to the accuracy with which FEERs can be diagnosed. The exercises presented in section 2 give no grounds for confidence that the "right" rate can be judged with any precision: it was suggested that they should be treated as having a margin of error of up to 10 percent. It would be misleading to identify a target zone narrower than the range of rates one is not prepared to label "clearly wrong," which suggests that target zones might initially be set at ± 10 percent. If the technical resources at the disposal of official institutions were brought to bear on making estimates of FEERs, it should be possible to improve on the exercises reported above and in consequence move to narrower zones. Another factor that might work in the same direction is any success that a more orderly exchange rate system has in curbing exchange rate swings: given the long lags in the adjustment of trade flows to exchange rates, a major uncertainty now facing balance of payments' econometricians is that of knowing what level of competitiveness should be credited with generating the observed current account outcomes.

Changing the Target Zone

Where the object of exchange rate management is to limit misalignments, target zones or central rates[25] will have to be changed to reflect differential inflation and changes in real exchange rates needed to promote adjustment. The only question is whether these changes should be made continuously in the light of accruing information or discontinuously as under the Bretton Woods system.

The latter alternative has nothing to commend it but nostalgia. Especially in a system of relatively narrow bands such as the EMS, the use of this antiquated practice virtually guarantees repeated exchange crises, of the character recently suffered by France, so long as significant differences in inflation rates persist. In its first two years (as in the final years of the snake) EMS realignments were small enough to be almost contained within the band, but they have recently been reaching levels of 8 percent or even 10 percent, with the predictable consequence of reviving exchange crises. There is no reason why differential inflation should not be neutralized by regular small changes in central rates (at, say, weekly intervals), according to a formula agreed six months or even a year in advance.

This amendment of EMS practice would in no way threaten the notable success that the EMS has enjoyed in forestalling intra-EMS misalignments of the type that have plagued the independently floating currencies. It would, admittedly, reduce the pressure that the EMS is supposed to create for a convergence in inflation rates, but it is not obvious that is a disadvantage, since the main reason for wanting inflation to be convergent— rather than low—is to enable the EMS to survive without exchange crises. Once that need were satisfied by the alternative route of adopting crawling central rates, each country would be freed to concentrate on reducing inflation to the lowest possible rate consistent with satisfactory performance of the real economy.

The need for crawling changes in the zone is less compelling in a target zone system. Nonetheless, it seems highly desirable to modify the target

---

25. Whether one names a central rate to a target zone, or simply the soft margins of such a zone, is a cosmetic question.

zone continuously in the light of the latest available information. That will require the use of "crawling zones."

Publication of Target Zones

Many officials still seem to take the view that, unless their country is to commit itself to a peg with formal margins, it is a matter of great importance that any exchange rate target they may have should be treated as a state secret. They remember the battles against speculators in the dying years of the Bretton Woods system, and witness with horror the continued struggle of the French authorities to keep the French franc in the EMS, and conclude that the way to avoid humiliation is to try to suppress any market knowledge of what they would like to see happen. They fear that any published target would become a "target to shoot at," and that if the rate moved outside the target zone it would serve to undermine their credibility.

There is a deep gulf on this issue between official and academic thinking. Thus the justification for official intervention offered by Michael Mussa (1981) is that it is a way for the authorities to guarantee their own honesty. Academic proponents of exchange rate targeting within a floating system— e.g., Ethier and Bloomfield (1975), with their reference rate proposal—have generally taken it for granted that a principal purpose of such a step would be to provide a focus for stabilizing speculation, which is possible only if the target is published. The problem that France has created for itself in the EMS arises not because it publishes the parity of the franc, but because it insists on the necessary changes in that parity being undertaken at lengthy intervals rather than in frequent small steps. Publication in itself encourages honesty and improves the information available to the market, which will be beneficial so long as policy is sensibly conducted. Indeed, one might judge whether policy is so conducted in part by its ability to withstand full disclosure and public debate.

It is surely true that many of the past examples of cases where the authorities have lost credibility as a result of their failure to achieve published targets have arisen through their becoming committed to inappropriate targets. In particular, any fixed nominal exchange rate eventually becomes an inappropriate target in the presence of differential inflation. Such situations would not arise under the type of system discussed above. But it is nonetheless possible that rates would at times stray outside target zones. The idea of "soft margins" is that the authorities should be prepared to accept such developments if they judge that to be wise. There can be no certainty that in particular instances that might not induce counterproductive psychological reactions in the markets. The best antidote is not, however, the defensive one of secrecy, but rather an honest attempt to explain what policy is and why it was adopted. The market may not always be immediately convinced, but, to the extent that the authorities have a coherent strategy that deserves to convince, one must surely believe that honesty will prove the best policy in the long run. A full target zone system should therefore provide for publication of the zones.

Policy Instruments

It has already been indicated that monetary policy should provide the main instrument to manage the exchange rate (which is *not* to argue that the exchange rate should be the exclusive, or even main, focus of monetary policy). There is not the slightest doubt that monetary policy provides a potent instrument for influencing the exchange rate: that is the valid central theorem of the "monetary approach to the balance of payments." It is more important to ask to what extent it is *desirable* to devote monetary policy to managing the exchange rate rather than to internal objectives, and whether there are other policy instruments that should also be directed in part to the task of exchange rate management.

Three observations may be made on the first issue. A first is that there is no point in trying to fine tune the exchange rate to a greater accuracy than one can hope to identify a misalignment. If the target zone is 20 percent wide because one lacks confidence in one's ability to identify the FEER to any greater degree of accuracy, it makes no sense to distort the monetary policy that would be preferred from a domestic standpoint in order to keep the exchange rate within some narrower range.

A second observation is that one's willingness to use policy—and that means essentially monetary policy, given what is argued about other instruments below—to manage the exchange rate should be the critical determinant of the choice between pegging the exchange rate within a formal band and floating with a target zone surrounded by soft margins. A band commits the authorities at a certain point to give primacy to the exchange rate commitment, whereas a target zone, as that term is being used here, means that a country's authorities retain the right to allow their internal objectives to override their exchange rate targets even in the event of a large misalignment. It is because it seems most unikely that the major countries, most especially the United States, would be willing to give primacy to exchange rate management over domestic monetary targeting in the foreseeable future that target zones constitute the strongest form of management that can be contemplated for the international monetary system at a global level.

A third observation is that willingness to direct monetary policy to achieving a target exchange rate will, and certainly should, depend upon the confidence that monetary policy elsewhere will be conducted responsibly. If its partner countries are in the habit of lurching from the use of monetary policy to "go for growth" to episodes of single-minded (and single-policy) anti-inflationism, a country will have a hard choice between following their lead and allowing exchange rate misalignments to emerge. Ideally, therefore, the establishment of target zones should be complemented by an agreement to coordinate monetary policies.[26]

Are there other policy instruments that could usefully complement monetary policy in keeping the exchange rate on track? One possibility is *sterilized intervention*,[27] which in principle—when assets are imperfect substitutes—gives a measure of freedom to influence the exchange rate independently of interest rates. However, the Jurgensen Report (1983) has now provided an authoritative endorsement of the view that has commanded increasing academic support in recent years: namely, that sterilized intervention is a useful tool for smoothing out short-run exchange rate volatility but virtually impotent to remedy persistent misalignments. Given that the major problem of floating rates is the size and persistence of misalignments rather than short-run volatility, one should not rely on much of a contribution from sterilized intervention.

While sterilized intervention by a single country may be a weak tool, it might have a role to play in the context of *coordinated intervention*. The markets may be impressed by a display that both parties agree that their bilateral rate is misaligned and are prepared to do something about it, even if one country (or even both countries) involved is reluctant to allow intervention to influence its domestic monetary policy. In general, however,

---

26. See McKinnon (1984) for elaboration of how this should be done.

27. Intervention in the exchange market is said to be "sterilized" when it is not allowed to affect the domestic money supply. This requires that the potential reduction in the monetary base as a result of the central bank selling foreign currency in exchange for domestic currency is prevented by a central bank purchase of domestic nonmonetary assets.

it is desirable that intervention be allowed to have some impact on the money supply: intervention that is less than fully sterilized is after all a way of systematically allowing the pursuit of an exchange rate target to have some influence on domestic monetary policy.

Another possible instrument is provided by *capital controls*. The attraction of capital controls is the same as that of sterilized intervention: that, if they can be made to work, they provide a degree of freedom to influence the exchange rate independently of interest rates. The use of capital controls has, however, been questioned both on the grounds of their doubtful effectiveness and their interference with an efficient allocation of capital. The question of effectiveness seems to vary a great deal between countries and over time. There *are* countries, of which the most notable example is Japan, that have had effective capital controls for lengthy periods. But there are also cases of countries (like the United States in the 1960s) that have employed capital controls that covered only certain types of transactions, which proved notably ineffective—not surprisingly, given that "money is fungible." Concerns about the inefficiencies of capital controls are sometimes rather exaggerated: it is, after all, perfectly possible to obtain major welfare gains by drawing on the international capital market to supplement domestic savings while controlling capital movements. Nevertheless, once a country has become well integrated into the world capital market, it would need pervasive controls to isolate it again. Such controls should not necessarily be ruled out under all circumstances, but they are not an attractive option to be deliberately embraced as a normal part of international monetary arrangements.

Another policy instrument that might be directed to influencing the exchange rate is *fiscal policy*. As the earlier discussion of the Feldstein doctrine illustrated, it is essential that fiscal policy be consistent with exchange rate policy. Nevertheless, fiscal policy is not well suited to be an instrument of exchange rate management, partly because it is too inflexible, and partly for the reason elaborated by Robert Mundell (1962)—namely, that fiscal policy has a "comparative advantage" in influencing domestic demand rather than the balance of payments, in comparison with monetary policy. Of course, both fiscal and monetary policy should in principle be determined simultaneously by a general equilibrium approach rather than by the "assignment" of each instrument to a single target, but it is helpful to think of the "structural" budget surplus reflecting various calls on savings and investment at a normal level of employment, while the actual budget surplus (or deficit) is allowed to vary over the cycle in the interests of stabilizing output.

A *Summary: The Characteristics of Target Zones*

While there has been scattered support in recent years for the notion of
"target zones," it has not been accompanied by any detailed exposition of
what would be involved in such an approach. As one unfortunate result,
target zones have been criticized as too rigid by some writers who were
clearly interpreting the idea in a far more rigid sense than that in which it
has been used here. It is hoped that the present attempt to give content to
the phrase will lead to future debate being directed at substance rather than
semantics.

As used here, the term "target zones" would involve:

● soft margins, rather than a commitment to prevent the rate from straying
outside the target zone

● a zone perhaps 20 percent wide, outside of which rates would be considered
"clearly wrong"

● a crawling zone, with the crawl reflecting both differential inflation and
any need for balance of payments adjustment

● publication of the target zone

● the partial direction of monetary policy (perhaps in the form of intervention
that is not fully sterilized) to discourage the exchange rate from straying
outside its target zone.

5   IMF Surveillance

Suppose that each individual country were to adopt the recommendations
made above: to estimate its FEER, adopt a target zone bounded by soft
margins around that rate, and intervene (while in general not fully sterilizing)
to discourage the market rate from straying beyond the target zone. Would
this produce a viable and consistent *system* of exchange rates for the world
economy?

There is one obvious but essential condition that would need to be satisfied to give an affirmative answer to that question. That condition is that the FEERs be mutually consistent. If that condition were not approximately[28] satisfied, the system would become an engine of inflation or deflation. Suppose, for example, that countries in general wished for more depreciated FEERs than was consistent with the choices being made by their partners, i.e., that there was a situation of incipient competitive depreciation. Then each country would be driven to a more expansionary monetary policy in the attempt to achieve its exchange rate target. To the extent that some countries succeeded in reaching their targets, others would find themselves frustrated and expand their money supplies in consequence. The result would be competitive monetary expansion and potentially an inflationary explosion. Conversely, if the FEER estimates were more appreciated than consistent with the choices of partners, there would be a threat of competitive monetary deflation.

It is therefore a matter of importance that the estimates of FEERs, which provide the central rates for target zones, be mutually consistent. One would obviously need some international mechanism to check for such consistency and to negotiate changes in target zones when it is lacking. The obvious organization to take on this task is the IMF, which would at last achieve a focus for its responsibilities for the surveillance of exchange rate policies that has been sadly lacking up to now. The "Versailles Group," consisting of the managing director of the Fund and representatives of the five major economic powers whose currencies constitute the SDR, would provide the natural forum for joint negotiation of target zones of the five major currencies.

How difficult would it be for the Fund to get its members to agree on a set of consistent estimates of FEERs? Only actual experience in seeking to negotiate an agreed set of target zones could give a conclusive answer to that question, but it is not obvious that such negotiations would usually be particularly difficult. Fundamentally, it is not clear why interests should be competitive rather than cooperative in regard to levels of real resource transfer. Empirically, the IMF ran a considerably more demanding par value system for over twenty years, with rather few symptoms of conflict over exchange

---

28. Given that target zones would be fairly wide and that countries' monetary policies would not be modified by exchange rate considerations until the rate approached the edge of the zone, there would be scope for quite a measure of inconsistency in central rates before the catastrophic consequences described in the text became a threat.

rate targets until the breakdown years of Bretton Woods. Even then, it is really not clear that there was much conflict over the substance of payments and exchange rate targeting, as opposed to posturing over "prestige" issues like who should take the initiative in proposing par value changes. In recent years one has not witnessed all countries simultaneously complaining that their currencies were overvalued or undervalued: on the contrary, the years of dollar overvaluation have produced vociferous complaints from both Germany and Japan that the DM and yen have been undervalued.

Nevertheless, there are circumstances where it might prove difficult to achieve agreement on target zones. The present (summer, 1983) provides a classic example. As discussed in section 2, current account targets and FEERs, and hence target zones, depend on the balance between savings and investment in a cyclically neutral situation. If the Fund passively accepted the looming US structural fiscal deficit, then it would be led to approve target zones based on a high value for the dollar and equivalently low values for other countries. Conversely, approval of target zones that reflect a desirable balance between domestic saving and investment in the United States would make sense only with accompanying action to reverse the impact of recent US fiscal policy. Thus implementation of a target zone approach would virtually force a serious international confrontation over US fiscal policy, rather than allowing international meetings to conclude with the sort of meaningless platitudes expressing agreement on abstract objectives that have become standard diplomatic practice.

Opinions will no doubt differ as to the implications. Some will surely argue that this consideration makes it unrealistic to contemplate a move toward a more structured exchange rate system, even of the rather loose form involved in a commitment to target zones. Others will point out that the problems that would make a diplomatic negotiation so difficult are not resolved by failing to confront them in international discussions, but instead jeopardize the performance of the world economy as long as they are allowed to fester. The fact is that the world is likely to continue to suffer from high real interest rates, low investment, an overvalued dollar, and all the consequences that flow from those distortions until the current budgetary profligacy is ended. If international pressure can hasten that day, any diplomatic unpleasantness that may be involved will be amply compensated.

Changing the focus of the Versailles Group, and of Fund surveillance in general, toward achieving agreement on target zones would represent a major break from the recent preoccupation with achieving "convergence." The choice of convergence as an objective is, however, fundamentally mistaken.

Convergence in inflation rates is unimportant; a *low* inflation rate is much to be desired, but its desirability is quite independent of the success that other countries are achieving in reducing inflation, provided that the exchange rate is managed (as it can be) to preserve competitiveness. Convergence in demand growth is in general positively harmful, for it implies international synchronization of the business cycle; and it is precisely that synchronization that gave us the 1973 acceleration of inflation and the devastating recessions of 1975 and 1980–83. Convergence in fiscal deflation in the middle of the deepest recession for a half-century made no sense whatever. Convergence in monetary growth makes sense only if it happens to induce a pattern of exchange rates consistent with the fundamentals. There is no sense in which convergence *per se* is a sensible goal.

There are, of course, *circumstances* in which convergent policies are desirable. If all countries were suffering from a large degree of slack and were free of inflation and balance of payments problems, then a concerted (convergent) expansion would be called for. Where there is a great deal of slack in the world economy but only a few countries strong enough to act as "locomotives," then parallel expansionary policies by those countries are desirable.[29] But the *objective* should be policies that are "compatible" or "consistent," which will only by accident prove to be convergent. And it is precisely the objective of compatibility on which attention would be focused by an attempt to negotiate a set of agreed target zones.

IMF surveillance would have a second aspect in addition to that of achieving agreement on a set of target zones. This would be to check that member countries gave proper attention to where their exchange rates lay relative to their target zones in implementing their economic policies, notably monetary policy. It is the essence of target zones, as opposed to bands around a formal peg, that countries not be required to defend the exchange rate margins rigidly. But it would make a mockery of the system if they ignored the agreed target zones in framing their monetary policy. The least that should be expected is that countries avoid intervention that would push their exchange rate away from their target zone, or keep them from moving toward the zone (even if "leaning against the wind"), and that policy not be more restrictive (expansionary) than would be justified by domestic needs when the currency

---

29. The program for a coordinated expansion published by the Institute for International Economics in December 1982 (Twenty-six Economists, 1982) called for five of the seven major economies to adopt more expansionary policies.

is appreciated above (depreciated below) its target zone. The Fund should be expected to supervise compliance with these minimum rules of behavior and to discuss with countries how far they go beyond that, in modifying the monetary policy they prefer on domestic grounds, with a view to limiting misalignments.

6   Conclusions

This study has argued that the great failing of floating rates is the large misalignments they have allowed to emerge. Misalignments, defined as deviations of the real exchange rate from the level of competitiveness needed in the medium term, jeopardize central dimensions of economic performance: they can result in a roller coaster of boom followed by austerity, unnecessary adjustment costs, unemployment in the tradable goods industries, deindustrialization, increased inflationary pressure, and protectionism. These misalignments may emerge either from market failure (inefficiencies in the foreign exchange market), or from policy failures (policy mixes chosen with no concern for their exchange rate consequences).

Misalignments can be identified, though admittedly not with any great precision. Misalignments are currently large, as they have been for much of the period of floating rates. It would therefore be highly desirable for governments, in consultation with the IMF, to set about seeking to identify the set of fundamental equilibrium exchange rates that would be appropriate from the standpoint of long-run competitive considerations. Ideally those FEERs might then become the central rates in a set of mutually consistent and publicly declared crawling target zones with soft margins, which countries would support by concerted intervention and, more important, by orienting their monetary policies in part to encouraging rates that stray outside the target zones to return toward them. Intervention policy would abandon its misconceived focus on "leaning against the wind" and concentrate instead on limiting misalignments.

A number of distinguished experts have in recent years advocated a position similar in central respects to that summarized above. Otmar Emminger (1982), Alexandre Lamfalussy (1981, 1983), and Anthony M. Solomon (1983) have all voiced their concern at the size of misalignments (without using the term);

expressed a conviction that it is at times possible to identify "clearly wrong" exchange rates; and called for policy adjustments to counter misalignments. Richard N. Cooper (quoted in *Business Week,* 27 June 1983, p. 100) and Robert V. Roosa (1983) have declared themselves in favor of moving toward a system of target zones. A recent report by the Working Group on International Monetary Affairs of the Atlantic Council of the United States (1983), the report on *International Monetary Arrangements* of the House of Commons Select Committee on the Treasury and Civil Service (1983, para. 5.7), and the report of a Commonwealth Study Group (1983, para. 3.41) have advocated versions of a target zone approach. So the ideas developed above are a more explicit, and in some respects more ambitious, version of a set of ideas that are beginning to gain influential support.

The international climate is currently hostile to grand international initiatives, to the point where even the limited steps advocated in this study may be regarded as unrealistic. But important progress might be achievable by more modest steps if there were general agreement that the underlying ideas are correct. The authorities might usefully start off by admitting to themselves that the exchange rate is a subject on which they *should* have a view. Central bankers might then start swapping those views among themselves to explore the measure of consistency that they could achieve. Where they found themselves in agreement among themselves but in disagreement with the market, they might experiment with joint intervention. Where a country found general sympathy with its own judgment that its exchange rate was misaligned, it might trim its monetary policy in an appropriate direction, using discretion as to the extent to which it reveals its motivation to the public.

Similarly, rather than start off with the idea of attempting to negotiate a complete set of target zones within the Versailles Group, the Group might agree that any member seriously out of current account balance be asked to file a letter explaining the reason for its situation and, where necessary, outlining its program to correct the imbalance.[30] A country might plead that its imbalance reflected a desirable capital flow, where considerations of the sort that should influence underlying capital flows (see section 2) can be shown to exist. Or it might argue that the imbalance was purely temporary,

30. A proposal along these lines was sketched by the US Secretary of the Treasury in his statement to the Annual Meetings of the International Monetary Fund and World Bank in 1979: see IMF (1979, p. 116).

either because the world had already changed or because the country had introduced—or was on the point of introducing—adjustment measures. Or perhaps the country would plead the Feldstein doctrine, that its imbalance was a part of a second-best solution. In any event, this procedure would provide a trial run for the sort of discussions that would be needed to agree a set of target zones, and it might also be an effective method of bringing major international inconsistencies in economic policy to the agenda in international discussions.

As and when such modest initiatives as these build up official confidence in the possibility and value of exchange rate management, one would hope to see support develop for a fully fledged target zone system. But, even short of that development, there is vast scope for improving the functioning of an exchange rate regime that has fallen far short of the hopes and expectations that accompanied its acceptance a decade ago.

7   Postscript

This postscript aims to do two things:

- to update the estimates of misalignments among the five major currencies
- to reassess the argument in favor of target zones in the light of subsequent developments—both intellectual and in the real world.

Updating has deliberately been restricted largely to the postscript, so as to leave the main text essentially as it was written in the summer of 1983. Amendments have been limited to correction of typographical errors, the occasional minor updating, and the employment of revised series for composite real effective exchange rates (REERs), due both to revisions in the original data series and to modifications in some of the computational techniques employed in the calculations.[31] The main change of substance is the omission of some qualms expressed in the first edition regarding what appeared to be

---

31. The most notable of these concerns a change in the algorithm used to translate changes in REERs into changes in bilateral exchange rates. This is now based directly on the inverse of the real version of the MERM.

TABLE 12   **Updated estimates of misalignments, 1984 Q4**

	Actual REER (1976–77 FEER = 100)	Changes in FEERs 1977–84 (percentage)	Effective exchange rate relative to estimated fundamental equilibrium[a]	Fundamental equilibrium rate against US dollar	Nominal appreciation needed against US dollar (percentage)
US dollar	142.8	+4	137	n.a.	n.a.
Japanese yen	91.8	+3	89	¥ 198	24
Deutschemark	85.1	−2	87	DM 2.04	50
French franc	91.3	−1	92	FF 6.51	44
Pound sterling	117.1	+9	107	$ 1.52	25
Other industrial country currencies	n.a.	n.a.	99[b]	n.a.	32[c]

n.a. Not applicable.
Sources: Tables 11 and A1.
a. Actual REER with 1984 Q4 FEER = 100.
b. Residual.
c. Unweighted mean.

a large implied overvaluation of the minor currencies. The numbers and figures in the appendix have been modified to reflect the revised data and have been updated to the end of 1984.[32]

Updated Estimates of Misalignments

My estimates of misalignments in the first quarter of 1983 were presented in table 11. Table 12 shows an updating of that table to the fourth quarter of 1984, using the same changes in FEERs over the period 1977–84 as were assumed in table 11 for 1977–83 except in two respects. One of these concerns the Japanese yen, whose FEER has been assumed to appreciate a further 2 percent on account of the productivity bias factor (p. 33).

The second concerns the US dollar and the Japanese yen, both of whose

---

32. The data are complete to the third quarter of 1984, but the updating to the fourth quarter is based on only five of the six series used to construct the composite index (and only two series for France).

FEERs are being significantly influenced by the changes in debt-service obligations generated by large current account imbalances. In 1983–84 the United States ran a deficit of $146 billion, and Japan a surplus of $57 billion.[33] Assuming a real interest rate of 5 percent, this implies that the United States must generate an additional surplus of $7.3 billion and permits Japan to reduce its surplus on other transactions by $2.9 billion, calling for depreciation of the dollar's FEER by 2 percent and appreciation of the yen's FEER by 3 percent, according to customary rules of thumb.

The striking feature of table 12, column 3, compared to table 11, is that, for all of the currencies but the pound, misalignment was even *larger* in the fourth quarter of 1984 than it had been in the first quarter of 1983. And even the pound was more undervalued on a bilateral basis vis-à-vis the dollar (final column). The biggest misalignment, that of the US dollar, was the one that increased the most.

My colleague Stephen Marris has raised an important criticism of my original analysis. He points out that one of the major countries, namely Japan, is being obliged to restrict (''voluntarily'') a wide range of exports to many major export markets. If those restraints were withdrawn, a further appreciation of the yen would be needed to offset the resulting increase in exports.

The question therefore arises of whether the definition of the fundamental equilibrium exchange rate should assume the withdrawal of such restraints, as it requires that a country not be ''restricting trade for balance of payments reasons'' (p. 14). If one can conceive of a policy package that includes both the correction of exchange rate misalignments and the withdrawal of such trade restraints, such an interpretation would seem eminently reasonable.

Unfortunately, however, there do not seem to be any comprehensive estimates of the impact of present restraints on the level of Japanese exports. Thus my estimate of the adjustment in the FEER that would be called for to allow for the withdrawal of these restraints has to be highly speculative. A 10 percent appreciation of the yen's FEER is adopted for illustrative purposes. According to the MERM (Artus and McGuirk 1981, p. 296), this appreciation would have been expected to decrease the Japanese trade balance by some $4.7 billion in 1977 (using the low-feedback parameters); scaling this up by

33. The question might be raised as to whether projected future deficits and surpluses should not also be taken into account, but this has not been done on the ground that such projections would inevitably be arbitrary.

TABLE 13   **Revised estimates of misalignments, 1984 Q4**

	Estimated REER (current FEER = 100)		Fundamental equilibrium rate against US dollar	
	Unadjusted	Adjusted for elimination of Japanese export restraints	Unadjusted	Adjusted for elimination of Japanese export restraints
US dollar	137	139	n.a.	n.a.
Japanese yen	89	81	¥ 198	¥ 182
Deutschemark	87	88	DM 2.04	DM 2.09
French franc	92	93	FF 6.51	FF 6.65
Pound sterling	107	108	$1.52	$1.49
Other industrial country currencies	99	99	32[a]	30[a]

n.a. Not applicable.
Sources: Table 12 and calculations described in text.
a. Unweighted average percentage appreciation against US dollar.

the subsequent growth in Japanese trade, one may estimate the present impact at around $10 billion.

Table 13 shows the effect of incorporating this modification into the updated estimates in table 12. The first and third columns reproduce the data in table 12, while the second and fourth have been adjusted for the elimination of Japanese export restraints.

Both sets of estimates are reproduced in the first two rows of table 14, where they are compared with estimates of medium-run exchange rate norms developed by other authors. Unfortunately these seem to be few and far between: I have located only five candidates:

- Armington Wolford and Associates publish a monthly newsletter dealing with exchange rate projections, based on a dynamic macroeconometric multicountry model. They calculate "medium-term norms" for the major currencies, defined as the geometric means of the monthly exchange rates forecast by their model for 72 months after the date of the forecast. These are the values shown in table 14. However, the authors have suggested that a conceptually more relevant comparison with my numbers would be the current values of the exchange rates on their steady-state trajectories.

TABLE 14   **Alternative estimates of medium-run exchange rate norms**

Source	Date to which estimates refer	Dollar: actual effective rate as percentage of norm	Norm for Japanese yen	Norm for Deutschemark	Norm for French franc	Norm for Pound sterling (dollar/ pound)
This study, with Japanese export restraints remaining	1984 Q4	137	198	2.04	6.51	1.52
This study, with $10 billion of Japanese export restraints removed	1984 Q4	137	183	2.08	6.64	1.49
Armington Wolford	1984 (Dec.)	147	131	1.93	6.99	1.57
Currency Research, Ltd.	1984 Q4	125	196	2.04	6.63	1.59
Marris	1984 Q4	145	—	—	—	—
MERM simulation	1985	149	160	2.02	6.50	1.80
OECD PPPs	1984 Q4	122[a]	209	2.33	6.74	1.82
Memorandum item						
Actual rate	1984 Q4	n.a.	246	3.05	9.36	1.22

— Not available.

n.a. Not applicable.

Sources: Table 13; Armington Wolford (1984); Currency Research (1985); Marris (forthcoming, 1985); McGuirk (personal communication); Hill (1984, table 2).

a. Trade-weighted average of overvaluation vis-à-vis 17 OECD currencies.

They plan to calculate such numbers, but none were available as this went to press.

• Currency Research, Ltd., a London-based company that specializes in the medium-term forecasting of exchange rates, uses as a major input to its forecasts the concept of a currency's "fundamental value." The *funda-*

mental value is defined as that exchange rate at which the overall balance of payments (including all capital movements with maturity greater than one year) would balance over time. It thus differs from the concept of a "fundamental equilibrium exchange rate" only in that the latter seeks to distinguish optimal from actual capital flows. The calculated fundamental values are changed by differential inflation, differential export sector productivity growth, and structural shifts due to factors like oil price changes, just as I argued FEERs would be. Table 14 shows estimates of fundamental values for the fourth quarter of 1984.

- My colleague Stephen Marris is completing a study entitled *Deficits and the Dollar: The World Economy at Risk* in which he calculates the dollar depreciation that would be needed to achieve specified levels of the current account deficit by 1990. My study assumed that a small ($12 billion per annum) current account deficit is an appropriate target for the United States (pp. 26, 33). Preliminary results from Marris' model indicate that the dollar would have to depreciate some 36 percent from its fourth quarter 1984 level to attain that deficit in 1990, i.e., that it was some 55 percent overvalued in nominal terms. Given the inflation feedback incorporated in his model, this implies a real overvaluation of 45 percent.

- Using the multilateral exchange rate model, Anne Kenny McGuirk has estimated the realignment that would be needed to secure a reduction of the US current account deficit by $80 billion. It is assumed that the counterpart of the improvement in the US current account would be declines in the current balances of Japan by $30 billion; Germany, $15 billion; France, $6 billion; and the United Kingdom, $4 billion. The remaining $25 billion is spread among the other industrial countries. No explicit allowance is made for the possibility that a growth catchup in Europe and Japan will contribute to an erosion of the US deficit, although one could argue that the relatively modest scale of the adjustment sought by exchange rate changes ("only" $80 billion) is consistent with some catchup.

- The Organization for Economic Cooperation and Development (OECD) recently published the results of a study of absolute purchasing power parities in its member countries. These are exchange rates that would equalize the ability to buy a defined basket of goods in different countries, and are therefore conceptually distinct from the exchange rates needed to produce some desired set of current account outcomes, which is what all the other approaches are seeking to identify. Nevertheless, there is a presumption that, among economies at a similar stage of development,

FEERs are unlikely to differ drastically from the rates that would equalize purchasing power parity, and hence it is of interest to compare the results of the OECD study with those yielded by alternative approaches.

In a thoughtful comment on my argument for target zones, Hans Genberg (1984) argued that the impossibility of achieving agreement among economists on appropriate values of FEERs would pose a major obstacle to adoption of the proposal. The comparisons shown in table 14 provide an opportunity to test the force of this argument. On first inspection, the numbers might seem to support his contention; the range of values (highest minus lowest) divided by their mean is 20 percent for the dollar, 43 percent for the yen, 19 percent for the deutschemark, 7 percent for the French franc, and 20 percent for the pound.

To some extent, however, different numbers can be explained as reflections of the different concepts being measured rather than as different evaluations of the same concept. For example, the Armington–Wolford estimates are based on a model with highly cyclical properties, which means that a period of (for example) dollar overvaluation in the recent past generates forecasts of a weak dollar in the future, and hence a low medium-run norm, relative to which the dollar appears more overvalued than it would relative to its steady-state value. Armington and Wolford plan to remedy this source of incomparability by estimating the steady-state characteristics of their model, but such estimates were not available as this postscript was concluded. Furthermore, unlike the other estimates shown in table 14, the Armington–Wolford figures show differences between current *nominal* exchange rates and medium-run norms, which one expects to be larger than the corresponding *real* misalignments because of the impact of exchange rate changes on price levels.

Another source of difference resides in the currency baskets used to calculate the dollar's effective exchange rate. In particular, Currency Research, Ltd., uses a wider currency basket, comprising 33 currencies covering 79 percent of US trade, whereas the other baskets include at most 17 currencies covering something over 50 percent of US trade. Since most of the additional currencies are those of new industrial countries that are closely tied to the dollar, it is to be expected that the dollar's overvaluation in terms of that wider basket will be less than that measured in terms of the other baskets.

Unlike the other approaches, that of Stephen Marris takes explicit account of the additional US debt that will be incurred before the US current account can be brought back into approximate balance. (My calculation allows for debt *already* incurred, but not for that which will be incurred in future: the implicit assumption is that the FEER is the exchange rate that would be needed if the system were capable of jumping directly to steady state. While this criterion is somewhat artificial, it is less arbitrary than any alternative, all of which require explicit assumptions about the *path* that adjustment will take—assumptions that Marris does indeed make.) It is to be expected that this will add to the size of the dollar overvaluation.

Finally, it was already pointed out above that the OECD study was seeking the answer to a rather different question, so that sizable deviations of those figures from the others should not be a cause for concern.

Readers will have to judge for themselves whether the differences between the various estimates are so substantial as to justify dismissing the possibility of achieving agreement on FEERs. The range of disagreement would in all cases seem to be narrowed by taking account of the points discussed above. In every case except that of the Japanese yen, the range of real disagreement appears to be well under 20 percent—the width projected for target zones—and probably under 10 percent.

In the case of the yen, however, there seems to be a real divergence of views on the order of 20 percent. High and low estimates appear to be distinguished by whether they look back to what would have been needed to achieve equilibrium in the past, or forward to what appears to be needed to achieve it in the future. One conjecture would be that the backward-looking estimates (my own and that of Currency Research, Ltd.) make insufficient allowance for the impact on trade of the continuing rapid supply-side expansion of the tradable goods sector of the Japanese economy (in the same way that estimates of the trade elasticities that ignored the supply side have system- atically overestimated the income elasticity of demand for Japanese exports: see Balassa, 1979). Until this question is satisfactorily resolved, my claim (p. 36) that reasonable modifications in the assumptions "would be unlikely to generate estimates that are more than 10 percent or so different from those presented in table 11" appears somewhat optimistic, but not so unrealistic as to justify dismissing the possibility of achieving agreement on FEERs.

The Case for Target Zones

The preceding calculations indicate that misalignments, especially of the dollar, became even more pronounced during the 18 months after publication of the first edition of this study than they had been before its publication. According to my calculations, the peak overvaluation of the dollar in late

February and early March 1985 was more than 40 percent, about as great as the peak overvaluation of sterling in late 1980 and about double the estimated overvaluation of the dollar which brought the collapse of the Bretton Woods system of fixed parities in the early 1970s. And my estimates are near the conservative end of the range reviewed above.

Most of the consequences that could be expected from such a massive overvaluation have indeed materialized. In particular, the US current account has gone into colossal deficit, which will make the United States the world's biggest net debtor by the end of 1985 and could take the debt/export ratio late in this decade to levels that usually trigger a debt crisis. With regard to deindustrialization, however, the United States has so far suffered less than did British manufacturing industry in 1980–81 (which is today perhaps 10 percent smaller than it would otherwise have been as a continuing legacy of the sterling overvaluation). The reason is that large parts of American industry have been able to replace production for the home and export markets lost to foreigners with defense production: the sectors where this substitution was not feasible (notably agriculture) have indeed been hit hard, as political pressures for protection or other relief demonstrate, but these sectors are comparatively few.

The longer the deficit persists, the greater the ultimate depreciation of the dollar will need to be, to service the foreign debt the United States is incurring (and greater still if the debt has to be repaid). At that time, the United States will bear a different subset of the costs discussed in section 3: austerity, adjustment costs to reverse some of the changes taking place today, and inflationary pressure. Subsequent events have done nothing to dictate a revision of my appraisal that these costs of misalignments can be extremely onerous.

Despite this, the official world has remained hostile to proposals for active exchange rate management. For example, on March 15, 1985, the US Treasury sent a report to Congress arguing that a target zone approach to exchange rate management was unnecessary because the "key to stable exchange rates is stable policies and policy expectations and more convergent economic performance in the major industrial countries" (US Treasury 1985, p. 13). Ironically, the 1985 *World Economic Outlook* published a month later took considerable satisfaction in the widespread adoption of what the IMF considers to be stable policies,[34] as well as the convergence of growth rates

---

34. "Governments for the most part have resisted pressures to resort to short-run stimulative policies and have opted instead to pursue steady growth with price stability, an approach that offers better prospects for sustained employment growth in the longer run." (IMF 1985, p. 28)

(p. 18) and inflation performance (p. 29). Yet both volatility and misalignments have almost certainly been greater than ever before in the first six months of 1985: indeed, in the two weeks after the Treasury report was sent to Congress, the dollar fell by over 8 percent against the European currency unit (ECU). According to press reports, the trigger for the dollar's decline was a run on privately insured savings and loan associations in Ohio.

The fact is that the key to stable exchange rates is policies that treat exchange rate stability as an important objective, not policies that remain unchanged when the market environment (including market psychology) changes. It is just not true, as the example of the local difficulties in Ohio showed once again, that the economic environment and market psychology will remain obligingly stable provided that economic policies are in some sense stable. There are after all numerous different senses in which policies could be stable, and no one would expect exchange rates to remain stable in some of those cases (for example, with constant nominal interest rates). In other cases, as with constant cyclically adjusted fiscal deficits and constant monetary growth, one might expect exchange rates to remain stable if shocks never originated from the private sector; but they do, witness Ohio. If one really considers stable exchange rates important, one needs policies whose predictability resides in their response to the behavior of exchange rates. That is what a target zone approach is intended to provide, though without the rigidity of a fixed band.

Some (but not all) critics of a target zone approach, including the US Treasury, seem to be under the impression that a target zone would be just another name for a wide band.[35] There are in fact two other differences between a wide band and a target zone besides the width of the zone:

- A target zone would be defined around a *real* exchange rate, thus preventing differential inflation alone from creating a need for adjustment of the target.

- A target zone would have soft margins, implying that a country's obligation would be to adjust policies so as to discourage a rate moving outside the zone or tend to push a rate outside the zone back toward it, not that it would be *obliged* to prevent the rate from straying outside the zone.

The last point leaves the door open for countries to give a strong weight

---

35. "Although the exchange rate band under a target zone system would be wider than under a fixed rate system, the principle is the same. Countries would still arbitrarily [*sic*] determine a 'correct' exchange rate or range of acceptable rates, which they then endeavor to enforce." (US Treasury 1985, p. 12)

to domestic objectives where these conflict with the medium-term norm for the exchange rate. The experience of the European Monetary System (which operates a band system) might make one wonder whether that much flexibility is necessary: the members have kept their exchange rates in line and have avoided major misalignments without the need for any conspicuous sacrifice of domestic objectives.[36] But the target zone approach is an attempt to introduce an element of concern for external factors into domestic policy making without any risk of making the external element dominant, motivated by the political judgment that this is the most internationalist solution that several of the major powers might be prepared to contemplate in the foreseeable future.

Could a target zone approach have helped to curb misalignments, given the limited nature of the obligations that it would have implied? To answer that question, one has to return to the issue of whether misalignments are caused by market inefficiency or by uncoordinated macroeconomic polices (pp. 49–55). If it was solely the latter, a target zone system would have been helpful only to the extent that it might have focused the minds of policymakers on the long-run disadvantages and dangers of the lopsided policy mixes they have pursued in recent years. That would have been constructive, but one may doubt that it would have been decisive.

In fact, it became increasingly difficult, as 1984 wore on, to explain the continuing surge of the dollar as a rational response of forward-looking markets using high real interest rates to discount back to the present from a viable long-run equilibrium rate. One alternative theory, advanced to explain the dollar's rise by the then Deputy Secretary of the US Treasury, held that portfolio preferences had shifted "toward investments in countries where the anticipated relative after-tax, real rate of return . . . is higher" (McNamar 1984, p. 4). The big snag with this theory is that the vast bulk of the capital inflow to the United States that has been bidding the dollar up (almost 80 percent in 1984[37]) went into financial instruments that earn a rate of interest, rather than into direct or equity investments that are presumably motivated directly by rates of return. (Of course, high rates of return might have helped

36. The possible exception concerns the French austerity moves of June 1982 and March 1983, which were explicitly motivated by the decision to remain in the EMS. However, the statement in the text remains justifiable if one takes the view that such measures would have been inevitable before long in any event, and that procrastination would merely have increased the ultimate cost of adjustment.
37. According to the Department of Commerce (BEA 85–11 of March 18, 1985), foreign direct investment in the United States in 1984 totaled $21.2 billion, and foreigners were net sellers of US stocks by $0.6 billion, out of total identified inward investment of $95 billion.

raise interest rates and in that way been instrumental in attracting a capital inflow, but this takes one back to the orthodox theory that McNamar was challenging.)

Another alternative theory is that a large part of international capital flows are insensitive to short-run expected exchange rate movements, because they consist of money that is being invested for lengthy periods, or because the decisionmaker involved is not exposed to exchange risk. Adherents of this view point to the foreign investments of Japanese life insurance companies or direct foreign investment in the first category, and to the lending decisions of US banks as examples of the second category. The large swing in the US capital account in recent years has in fact occurred in US bank lending, which swung from a net outflow of over $40 billion in 1981–82 to a net inflow of over $20 billion in 1983–84. The basic problem may then be one of inadequate capital that is sensitive to the expected short-run relative profitability of investment in different currencies, so allowing exchange rates to swing erratically around equilibrium values.

Yet another alternative theory, whose chief adherent seems to be President Reagan, holds that investors are motivated by a desire to register their confidence in a country's policies rather than to make money. Embarrassing as it may be for the economics profession, this theory does seem more consistent with accounts of what drove the markets in late 1984 and early 1985 than our standard models. But despite this most of us would be loath to endorse the theory. A more congenial solution is to postulate that, while each individual market operator remains motivated by pecuniary self-interest, each of them also recognizes that the way to make money is to anticipate what the market will do, and each believes *others* to be over-impressed by confidence factors. That takes us right back to Keynes' analogy with a beauty contest, recalled on p. 53 above.

One of the consequences of a market in which individual operators condition their actions on their view of what they think others will do is the possibility of speculative bubbles (Hahn 1984, p. 124). Events since publication of the first edition of this study suggest that this possibility has to be taken even more seriously than it was on pp. 51–53. Few even tried to argue that the heights to which the dollar rose in late 1984 and early 1985 could be justified as a rational response to the high real interest rates that could be expected for an interim period prior to the exchange rate returning to a plausible long-run equilibrium level.[38] Instead, the story told in the

---

38. Marris (forthcoming, 1985) presents detailed projections establishing the implausibility of any such contention.

markets was that the dollar was expected to rise even more before it started its inevitable decline. Only the then Deputy Secretary of the US Treasury seemed to harbor the illusion that no such decline need ever occur:

Turning to debt, overseas investors have shown the same eagerness for corporate dollar denominated bonds. . . . Is it the nominal interest rate differentials or the currency appreciation potential on the principal that attracts them? I would suggest that . . . the latter consideration . . . is often of paramount importance to the foreign investor. (McNamar 1984)

Thus, the anxiety to show that the dollar was not overvalued because of excessively high interest rates led Treasury spokesmen into arguing that it was strong because it was expected to become ever more overvalued in the future!

If exchange markets are in fact driven by beliefs that the unsustainable will last forever, or even by widespread faith in the possibility of getting out before the average investor when the bubble bursts, the case for conscious exchange rate management is overwhelming. For the question is then not whether it is better to allow shocks generated in the private sector to be wholly absorbed by the exchange rate rather than partly or wholly absorbed elsewhere, as portrayed by Murphy (1985), but whether to tolerate the independent generation of additional shocks in the foreign exchange market.

One may still hope that the US administration will come to recognize the importance of bringing the dollar down to a sensible level without provoking a loss of confidence and a new overshooting. Should it do so, the rational way to go about the task would be to combine an assault on the budget deficit with the promulgation of a target zone for the dollar (preferably after consultation with the IMF). Both elements are essential. Announcement of a target zone, backed by intervention to correct the dollar and a relaxation of monetary policy, could reignite inflation if it was not accompanied by major action on the fiscal front. Conversely, a cut in the budget deficit could conceivably strengthen the dollar unless it were accompanied by a clear statement, backed up by policy actions (pp. 69–72), that the authorities recognized that the dollar had been too strong and were intent on restoring it to an appropriate level based on long-run competitiveness considerations.

Concluding Comments

The first part of this postscript updated my estimates of currency misalignments and compared them with alternative attempts to take a view of appropriate medium-run exchange rate norms. These calculations suggested that misalignments had increased substantially since the first edition of the monograph, while the comparisons suggested that—except for the yen—there was a reasonable degree of agreement as to the correct value of the FEER. The second part of the postscript argued that a major reason for the enlarged misalignments appears to lie in larger deviations of market equilibrium from current equilibrium, i.e., in market irrationalities. In toto, one might conclude that, while implementation of a target zone approach might be somewhat more difficult than I had portrayed it, the successful adoption of such an approach would offer even bigger benefits.

This conclusion suggests that the possibility of initiating steps toward a target zone system on a more limited and experimental basis than is recommended above may be worth exploring, if nothing more extensive can be negotiated in the near term. One idea (due to Paul Armington) is that the IMF might be instructed to start calculating a set of FEERs, and publishing them in *International Financial Statistics*. The aim would be not just to provide a practical test of the feasibility of providing estimates of the type that would be essential to implement a target zone system, but also to meet the clear and present worldwide need, felt by budgeting, planning, and contracting departments of a host of organizations engaged in continuing international transactions, for valid estimates of exchange rates sustainable in the medium term. This is the minimal step that those dissatisfied with the operation of floating exchange rates should seek in the immediate future.

References

Ardito-Barletta, Nicholas, et al. 1983. *Economic Liberalization and Stabilization Policies in Argentina, Chile, and Uruguay: The Monetary Approach to the Balance of Payments.* Washington: World Bank.

Armington, Paul S. 1981. "A Closed, Multilateral Model of the International Adjustment Process, With No Sectoral Disaggregation." Paper presented to the International Workshop on Exchange Rates in Multicountry Econometric Models, University of Leuven, Belgium. Processed.

Armington, Paul S., and Catherine Wolford. 1983. "A Model-Based Analysis of Dollar Fluctuations." Paper presented to the Third International Symposium on Forecasting, June, Philadelphia. Processed.

Armington Wolford & Associates. 1984. *Monthly Newsletter* (11 December).

Artus, Jacques R., and Anne Kenny McGuirk. 1981. "A Revised Version of the Multilateral Exchange Rate Model." *IMF Staff Papers.* June.

Atlantic Council of the United States. 1983. *The International Monetary System: Exchange Rates and International Indebtedness.* Policy study of the Working Group on International Monetary Affairs. Washington.

Balassa, Bela. 1964. "The Purchasing Power Parity Doctrine: A Reappraisal." *Journal of Political Economy,* vol. 72, no. 6 (December).

————. 1979. "Export Composition and Export Performance in the Industrial Countries, 1953–71." *Review of Economics and Statistics,* vol. 615, no. 4 (November).

Begg, David K. H. 1982. *The Rational Expectations Revolution in Macroeconomics: Theories and Evidence.* Deddington, Oxon: Philip Allan.

Bergsten, C. Fred. 1982. "What To Do About the US-Japan Economic Problem." *Foreign Affairs,* vol. 60, no. 5 (Summer).

Bergsten, C. Fred, and John Williamson. 1983. "Exchange Rates and Trade Policy." In *Trade Policy in the 1980s,* ed. William R. Cline. Washington: Institute for International Economics.

Business Week. 27 June 1983.

Clark, Peter B., and C. Haulk. 1972. "Flexible Exchange Rates and the Level of Trade: A Preliminary Analysis from Canadian Experience." Board of Governors of the Federal Reserve System, Washington. Processed.

Coes, Donald V. 1981. "The Crawling Peg and Exchange Rate Uncertainty." In *Exchange Rate Rules,* ed. John Williamson. London: Macmillan, and New York: St. Martin's Press.

Commonwealth Study Group. 1983. *Towards a New Bretton Woods: Challenges for the World Financial and Trading System.* London: Commonwealth Secretariat.

Currency Research, Ltd. 1985. "Fundamental Values of Major Currencies." London. Processed. April.

Cushman, David O. 1983. "The Effects of Real Exchange Rate Risk on International Trade." *Journal of International Economics,* vol. 15 (August).

Diaz-Alejandro, Carlos F. 1976. *Foreign Trade Regimes and Economic Development: Colombia.* New York: NBER.

Dornbusch, Rudiger. 1976. "Expectations and Exchange Rate Dynamics." *Journal of Political Economy,* vol. 84, no. 6 (December).

———. "Flexible Exchange Rates and Interdependence." 1983. *IMF Staff Papers.* May.

Emminger, Otmar. 1982. *Exchange Rate Policy Reconsidered.* Group of Thirty Occasional Paper, no. 10. New York.

Ethier, Wilfred, and Arthur I. Bloomfield. 1975. *Managing the Managed Float.* Essays in International Finance, no. 112. Princeton, NJ: Princeton University.

Feldstein, Martin. 1983a. "Is the Dollar Overvalued?" Speech Before the Council on Foreign Relations, April, New York. Processed.

———. "The World Economy Today." 1983b. *The Economist,* vol. 287, no. 7293. 11 June.

Forsyth, P. J., and John A. Kay. 1980. "The Economic Implications of North Sea Oil." *Fiscal Studies,* no. 1.

Genberg, Hans. 1984. "On Choosing the Right Rules for Exchange–Rate Management." *The World Economy,* vol. 7, no. 4 (December).

Goldstein, Morris. 1980. *Have Flexible Exchange Rates Handicapped Macroeconomic Policy?* Princeton Special Papers in International Economics, no. 14. Princeton, NJ.

Haberler, Gottfried. 1983. "The International Monetary System in the World Recession." In *Contemporary Economic Problems, 1983–84,* ed. William J. Fellner. Washington: American Enterprise Institute.

Hahn, Frank. 1984. "Reflections on the Invisible Hand" (reprint of his Fred Hirsch Memorial Lecture). In *Equilibrium and Macroeconomics.* Oxford: Blackwell.

Hause, J. C. 1966. "The Welfare Costs of Disequilibrium Exchange Rates." *Journal of Political Economy,* vol. 74, no. 4 (August).

Hill, Peter. 1984. "Real Gross Product in OECD Countries and Associated Purchasing Power Parities." *OECD Working Paper,* no. 17. December.

Hooper, Peter, and S. W. Kohlhagen. 1978. "The Effects of Exchange Rate Uncertainty on the Prices and Volume of International Trade." *Journal of International Economics,* vol. 8, no. 4.

House of Commons Select Committee on the Treasury and Civil Service. 1983. *International Monetary Arrangements.* London: Her Majesty's Stationery Office.

IMF. 1970. *The Role of Exchange Rates in the Adjustment of International Payments: A Report by the Executive Directors.* Washington.

———. 1979. *Summary Proceedings of the Thirty-fourth Annual Meeting of the Board of Governors.* Washington.

———. 1983. *Annual Report on Exchange Arrangements and Exchange Restrictions.* Washington.

———. 1985. *World Economic Outlook.* Washington. April.

Johnson, Harry G. 1966. "The Welfare Costs of Exchange Rate Stabilization." *Journal of Political Economy,* vol. 74, no. 5.

———. 1969. "The Case for Flexible Exchange Rates, 1969." In H. G. Johnson and J. Nash, *UK and Floating Exchanges.* London: Institute for Economic Affairs.

Jurgensen Report. 1983. *Report of the Working Group on Exchange Market Intervention.* Washington: US Treasury.

Kenen, Peter B., and Clare Pack. 1980. *Exchange Rates, Domestic Prices, and the Adjustment Process.* Group of Thirty Occasional Paper, no. 1. New York.

Kenen, Peter B., and Dani Rodrik. 1983. "Measuring and Analyzing the Effects of Short-term Volatility in Real Exchange Rates." Princeton, NJ: Princeton University. Processed.

Keynes, John Maynard. 1936. *The General Theory of Employment, Interest and Money.* London: Macmillan.

Kohlhagen, Steven W. 1982. In C. Fred Bergsten, et al. *From Rambouillet to Versailles: A Symposium.* Essays in International Finance, no. 149. Princeton, NJ: Princeton University.

Kuran, Timur. 1983. "Asymmetric Price Rigidity and Inflationary Bias." *American Economic Review,* vol. 73, no. 3 (June).

Lamfalussy, Alexandre. 1981. "A Plea for an International Commitment to Exchange Rate Stability." Paper presented at the 20th Anniversary Meeting of the Atlantic Institute for International Affairs, Brussels. Processed.

————. 1983. "Some General Policy Considerations for Tempering the Excesses of Floating." Paper presented to a *Financial Times* conference, 16 February. London. Processed.

McGuirk, Anne Kenny. 1983. "Oil Price Changes and Real Exchange Rate Movements among Industrial Countries." *IMF Staff Papers.* December.

McKinnon, Ronald I. 1984. *An International Standard for Monetary Stabilization.* POLICY ANALYSES IN INTERNATIONAL ECONOMICS 8. Washington: Institute for International Economics. March.

McNamar, R. T. 1984. Remarks before the Financial Executives Institute at New Orleans, Louisiana. US Treasury press release R–2876. 8 October.

Magee, Stephen P. 1972. "The Welfare Effects of Restrictions on US Trade." *Brookings Papers on Economic Activity,* no. 3.

Makin, John H. 1976. "Eurocurrencies and the Evolution of the International Monetary System." In *Eurocurrencies and the International Monetary System,* ed. Carl H. Stein, John H. Makin, and Dennis E. Logue. Washington: American Enterprise Institute.

Marris, Stephen. 1985. *Deficits and the Dollar: The World Economy at Risk.* Washington: Institute for International Economics. Forthcoming.

Mayer, Helmut, and Hiroo Taguchi. 1983. *Official Intervention in the Exchange Markets: Stabilising or Destabilising?* Basle: Bank for International Settlements.

Mundell, Robert A. 1962. "The Appropriate Use of Monetary and Fiscal Policy under Fixed Exchange Rates." *IMF Staff Papers.* March.

Murphy, J. Carter. 1985. "Reflections on the Exchange Rate System." *American Economic Review,* vol. 75, no. 2 (May).

Mussa, Michael. 1981. *The Role of Official Intervention.* Group of Thirty Occasional Paper, no. 6. New York.

Nurkse, Ragnar. 1944. *International Currency Experience.* Geneva: League of Nations.

Richardson, J. David. 1982. "The New Nexus Among Trade, Industrial, and Exchange Rate Policies." Paper prepared for presentation at a conference on the Future of the International Monetary System, cosponsored by New York University, the University of Southern California, and Tel-Aviv University, 7–8 October, New York. Processed.

Roosa, Robert V. 1983. "How to Create Exchange Rate Target Zones." *Journal of Commerce.* 3 June.

Schulmeister, Stephan. 1983. "Exchange Rates, Prices and Interest Rates." New York: New York University. Processed.

Shafer, Jeffrey R., and Bonnie E. Loopesko. 1983. "Floating Exchange Rates After Ten Years." *Brookings Papers on Economic Activity.* Washington: Brookings Institution.

Solomon, Anthony M. 1983. "Toward Realistic Cooperation." In G. de Menil and A. M. Solomon, *Economic Summitry.* New York: Council on Foreign Relations.

Taylor, Dean. 1982. "Official Intervention in the Foreign Exchange Market, or Bet Against the Central Bank." *Journal of Political Economy,* vol. 90, no. 2 (April).

Twenty-six Economists. 1982. *Promoting World Recovery: A Statement on Global Economic Strategy.* Washington: Institute for International Economics.

US Treasury. 1985. *Report to the Congress on the Functioning of the International Monetary and Financial System and the Role and Operation of the International Monetary Fund.* Washington. 15 March.

Williamson, John. 1982. "A Survey of the Literature on the Optimal Peg." *Journal of Development Economics,* vol. 11 (September).

———. 1983. *The Open Economy and the World Economy.* New York: Basic Books.

Appendix

TABLE A1   **Composite measure of real effective exchange rates**
(1976–77 FEER = 100)

	United States	Japan	United Kingdom	Germany	France
1970 Q1	140.2	81.3	102.9	87.4	98.2
Q2	139.1	81.4	103.5	87.4	98.2
Q3	137.5	81.3	104.5	87.8	98.1
Q4	136.7	80.4	105.7	88.4	98.0
1971 Q1	135.9	79.2	108.0	88.8	98.1
Q2	134.5	78.5	109.0	89.6	98.1
Q3	131.7	79.1	109.2	92.7	95.9
Q4	127.0	82.7	109.5	92.7	94.5
1972 Q1	122.2	85.7	111.0	92.2	97.7
Q2	121.0	85.8	109.6	92.3	99.3
Q3	120.4	86.7	104.3	92.2	99.8
Q4	119.6	88.5	102.0	91.4	100.1
1973 Q1	115.0	93.1	98.6	94.6	100.1
Q2	108.2	96.7	97.9	98.5	104.0
Q3	102.7	95.1	91.3	108.1	104.3
Q4	104.6	98.3	91.4	103.9	102.3
1974 Q1	108.9	100.0	91.6	102.8	95.7
Q2	102.4	103.8	94.3	105.3	92.2
Q3	105.2	98.4	97.1	100.3	97.1
Q4	105.1	94.8	98.9	99.7	99.2
1975 Q1	100.7	92.4	100.1	101.6	101.7
Q2	100.1	90.5	102.6	98.0	108.6
Q3	103.8	91.7	102.4	93.4	108.8
Q4	105.7	90.9	101.6	91.7	108.3
1976 Q1	106.0	91.2	102.1	93.1	108.8
Q2	107.2	92.0	94.1	96.0	107.6
Q3	105.7	94.1	93.6	96.4	102.4
Q4	105.9	92.4	87.1	99.8	100.4
1977 Q1	106.0	93.7	92.6	99.4	99.4
Q2	104.8	95.7	94.6	99.3	99.3
Q3	103.8	97.4	96.1	99.4	100.6
Q4	101.8	102.0	99.8	100.2	99.7
1978 Q1	99.3	100.4	103.4	102.4	96.8
Q2	98.6	106.1	98.8	102.1	100.2

	United States	Japan	United Kingdom	Germany	France
1978 Q3	94.4	116.6	101.2	99.3	103.0
Q4	93.2	113.3	103.7	103.0	101.9
1979 Q1	94.4	104.6	106.9	104.0	103.2
Q2	96.9	96.8	114.1	101.7	103.4
Q3	94.6	93.7	122.6	102.4	103.1
Q4	96.3	84.5	120.9	104.6	106.8
1980 Q1	97.3	81.9	129.5	103.4	107.4
Q2	97.7	85.7	134.8	100.9	107.1
Q3	95.3	88.3	140.7	99.5	107.8
Q4	97.7	93.4	147.5	95.2	106.0
1981 Q1	102.8	97.6	151.1	90.4	103.3
Q2	110.5	95.2	143.9	89.9	99.7
Q3	116.5	93.0	133.3	88.7	100.8
Q4	112.8	90.9	131.6	92.0	100.6
1982 Q1	116.9	88.2	134.7	90.1	100.1
Q2	120.3	86.0	134.0	91.6	99.7
Q3	124.9	82.5	134.4	92.3	93.9
Q4	126.8	83.1	131.3	92.6	94.1
1983 Q1	122.9	89.6	118.4	92.7	96.6
Q2	124.4	89.9	125.8	91.8	92.7
Q3	127.8	89.3	126.3	89.8	91.8
Q4	129.0	92.4	125.1	89.1	91.5
1984 Q1	130.0	93.1	123.7	89.3	90.6
Q2	130.9	93.7	121.8	88.5	92.3
Q3	138.1	91.3	120.1	86.4	91.3
Q4	142.8	91.8	117.1	85.1	91.3

Source: See footnote 9, p. 18, in text.

FIGURE A1   **Alternative measures of real effective exchange rates, United States**

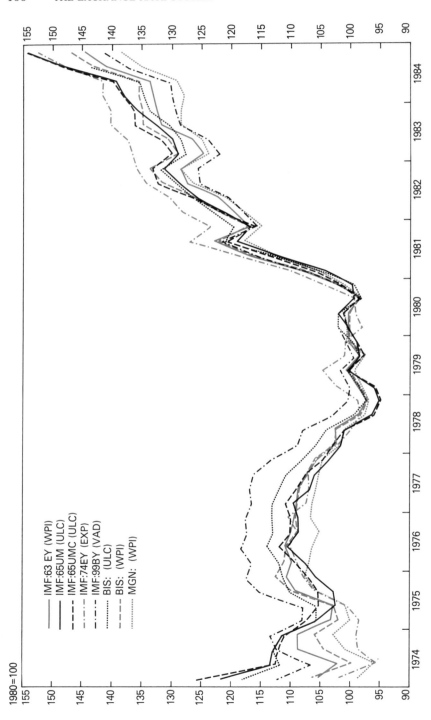

1980=100

IMF:63 EY (WPI)
IMF:65UM (ULC)
IMF:65UMC (ULC)
IMF:74EY (EXP)
IMF:99BY (VAD)
BIS: (ULC)
BIS: (WPI)
MGN: (WPI)

Note: Series are based on the following indices: wholesale prices (WPI); unit labor costs (ULC); export unit values (EXP); and value-added deflators (VAD).

Sources: International Monetary Fund, Bank for International Settlements, and Morgan

FIGURE A2 **Alternative measures of real effective exchange rates, Japan**

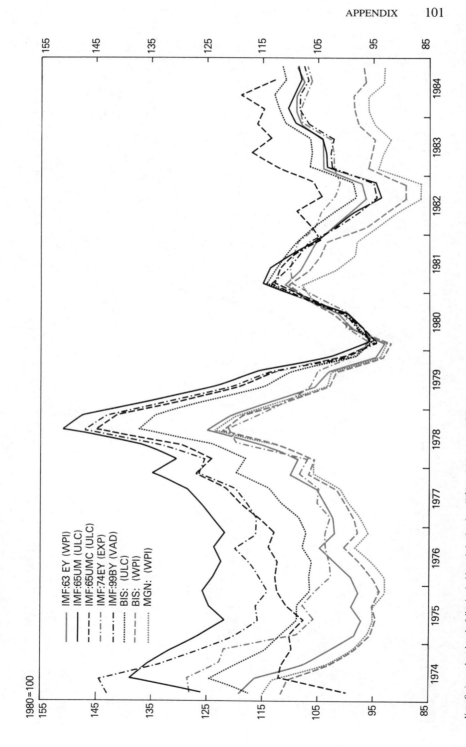

1980=100

IMF:63 EY (WPI)
IMF:65UM (ULC)
IMF:65UMC (ULC)
IMF:74EY (EXP)
IMF:99BY (VAD)
BIS: (ULC)
BIS: (WPI)
MGN: (WPI)

Note: Series are based on the following incides: wholesale prices (WPI); unit labor costs (ULC); export unit values (EXP); and value-added deflators (VAD).
Source: See figure A1.

FIGURE A3   **Alternative measures of real effective exchange rates, Germany**

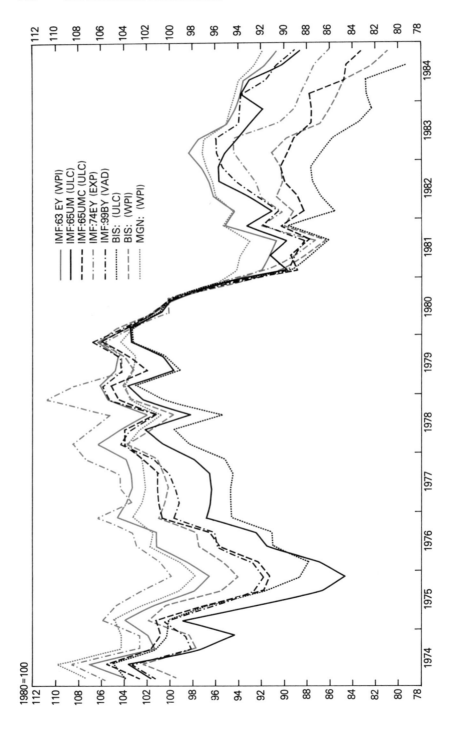

Note: Series are based on the following indices: wholesale prices (WPI); unit labor costs (ULC); export unit values (EXP); and value-added deflators (VAD).
Source: See figure A1.

FIGURE A4 **Composite measures of real effective exchange rates, five major countries**

1976-77 Fundamental equilibrium exchange rate =100

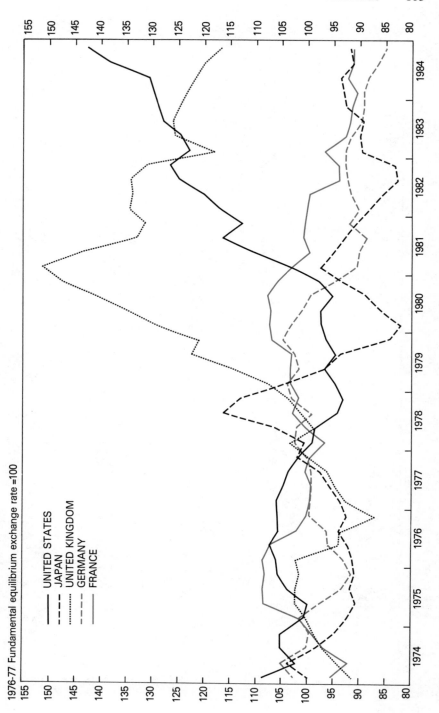

UNITED STATES
JAPAN
UNITED KINGDOM
GERMANY
FRANCE

Source: See footnote 9, p. 18.

FIGURE A5 **Decomposition of changes in US real effective exchange rate**

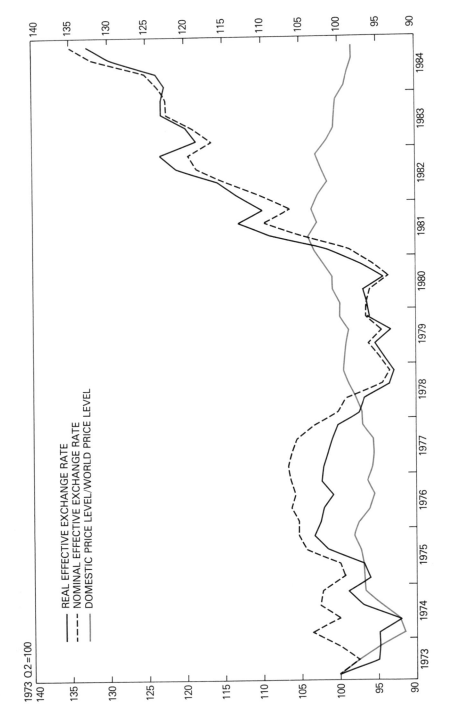

1973 Q2=100

REAL EFFECTIVE EXCHANGE RATE
NOMINAL EFFECTIVE EXCHANGE RATE
DOMESTIC PRICE LEVEL/WORLD PRICE LEVEL

Source: World Financial Markets, various issues.

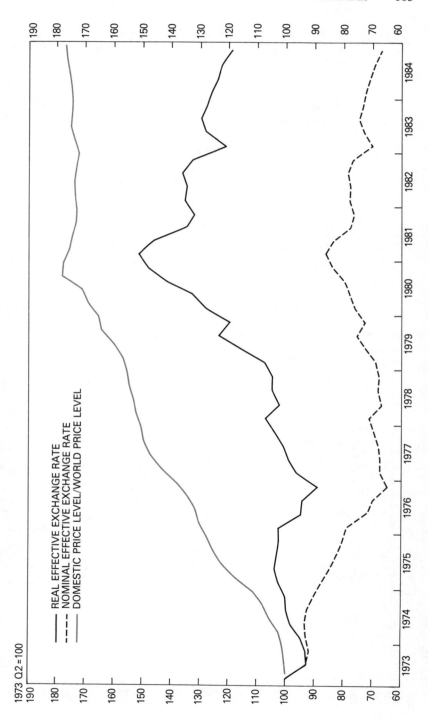

FIGURE A6 **Decomposition of change in UK real effective exchange rate**

1973 Q2=100

REAL EFFECTIVE EXCHANGE RATE
NOMINAL EFFECTIVE EXCHANGE RATE
DOMESTIC PRICE LEVEL/WORLD PRICE LEVEL

Source: World Financial Markets, various issues.

FIGURE A7 **Composite real effective exchange rate, United States (with 20 percent zone)**

Avg. 1976-77 Fundamental equilibrium exchange rate=100

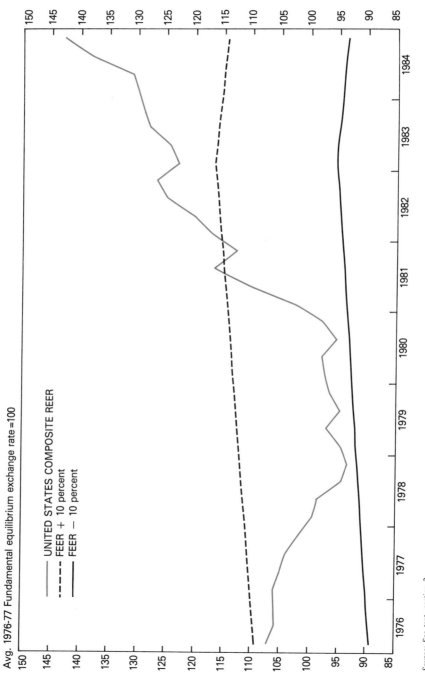

UNITED STATES COMPOSITE REER

FEER + 10 percent

FEER − 10 percent

Source: See text, section 2.

FIGURE A8 **Composite real effective exchange rate, Japan (with 20 percent zone)**

Avg. 1976-77 Fundamental equilibrium exchange rate=100

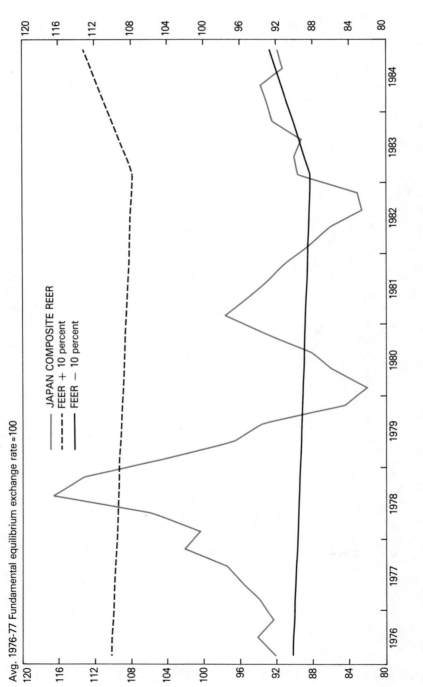

Source: See text, section 2.

FIGURE A9 **Composite real effective exchange rate, Germany (with 20 percent zone)**

Avg. 1976-77 Fundamental equilibrium exchange rate = 100

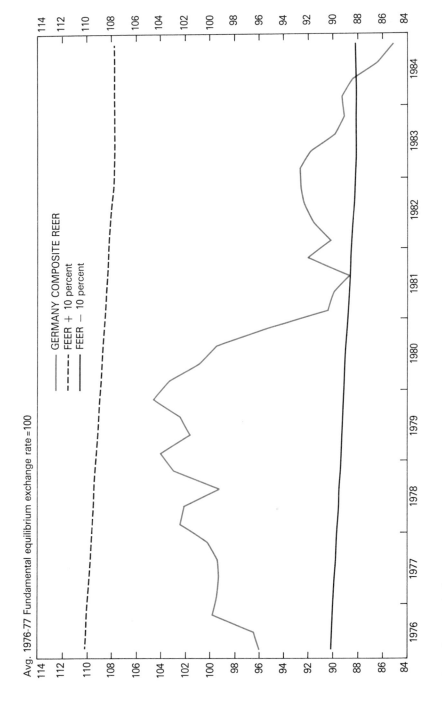

——— GERMANY COMPOSITE REER
------ FEER + 10 percent
——— FEER − 10 percent

FIGURE A10 **Composite real effective exchange rate, France (with 20 percent zone)**

Avg. 1976-77 Fundamental equilibrium exchange rate =100

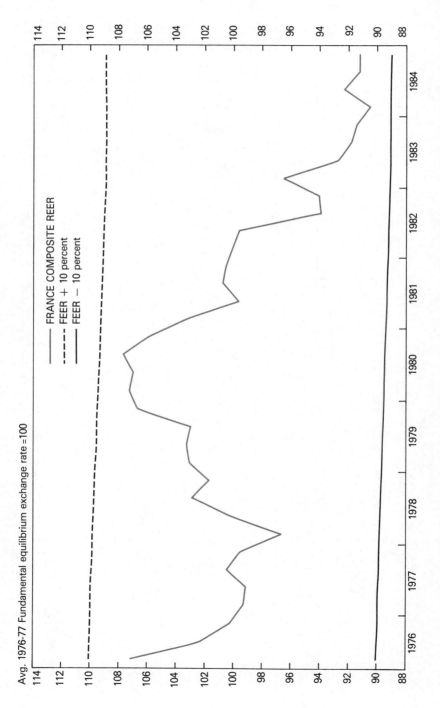

FRANCE COMPOSITE REER
FEER + 10 percent
FEER − 10 percent

Source: See text, section 2.

FIGURE A11 **Composite real effective exchange rate, United Kingdom (with 20 percent zone)**

Avg. 1976-77 Fundamental equlibrium exchange rate=100

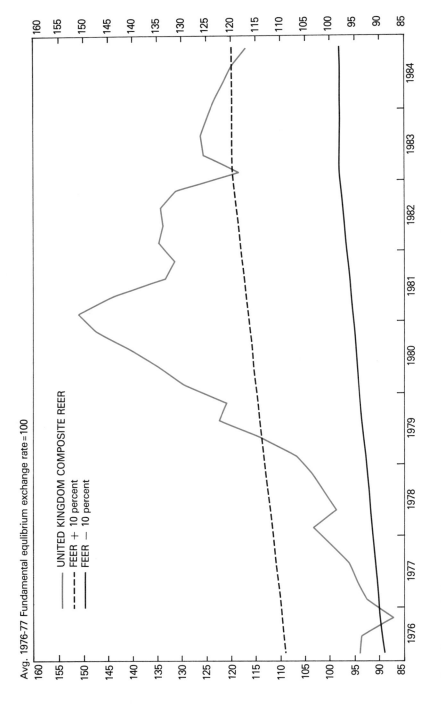

Source: See text, section 2.